NANCY ZIEMAN'S

Sewing A to Z

YOUR SOURCE for SEWING and QUILTING TIPS and TECHNIQUES

Nancy Zieman

Krause Publications
CINCINNATI, OHIO

Nancy Zieman's Sewing A to Z. Copyright © 2011 by Nancy Zieman. Manufactured in China. All rights reserved. No part of this book may be reproduced in any form or by any electronic or mechanical means including information storage and retrieval systems without permission in writing from the publisher, except by a reviewer who may quote brief passages in a review. Published by Krause Publications, a division of F+W Media, Inc., 4700 East Galbraith Road, Cincinnati, Ohio, 45236. (800) 289-0963. First Edition.

15 14 13 12 11   5 4 3 2 1

www.fwmedia.com

DISTRIBUTED IN CANADA BY FRASER DIRECT
100 Armstrong Avenue
Georgetown, ON, Canada L7G 5S4
Tel: (905) 877-4411

DISTRIBUTED IN THE U.K. AND EUROPE BY F&W MEDIA INTERNATIONAL
Brunel House, Newton Abbot, Devon, TQ12 4PU, England
Tel: (+44) 1626 323200, Fax: (+44) 1626 323319
Email: enquiries@fwmedia.com

DISTRIBUTED IN AUSTRALIA BY CAPRICORN LINK
P.O. Box 704, S. Windsor NSW, 2756 Australia
Tel: (02) 4577-3555

ISBN 13: 978-1-4402-1429-5
SRN: Y0005

Edited by *Kelly Biscopink*

Designed by *Julie Barnett*

Production coordinated by *Greg Nock*

Photography by *Al Parrish and Dale Hall*

Illustrations by *Laure Noe*

Nancy's Notions editorial staff: *Diane Dhein and Pat Hahn*

metric conversion chart

TO CONVERT	TO	MULTIPLY BY
inches	centimeters	2.54
centimeters	inches	0.4
feet	centimeters	30.5
centimeters	feet	0.03
yards	meters	0.9
meters	yards	1.1

Measurements have been given in imperial inches with metric conversions in brackets—use one or the other as they are not interchangeable. The most accurate results will be obtained using inches.

About the Author

Nancy Zieman is executive producer and host of Public TV's *Sewing With Nancy*, where she has been teaching viewers the art of sewing, quilting and embroidering since 1982. She also founded Nancy's Notions, a mail-order and online source for sewing and quilting products. As one of the sewing industry's most trusted voices, she has been honored and celebrated by organizations from the National 4-H Club to the American Sewing Guild. So wherever you see a *Note from Nancy*, you'll know you're getting expert advice!

ACKNOWLEDGMENTS

As the figurehead of a TV show and direct mail company, I tend to receive undeserved accolades for the successes of both entities. The proverb that includes the words "it takes a village" applies to life in general. My village is a tight-knit group of people who have worked with me over many decades.

My TV program should really be called *Sewing With Nancy, Donna, Pat, Laure, Kate, Diane D., Diane S., Deanna, Lois, Gail and Erica*. They comprise the dedicated village that shares a love of sewing and quilting. To them I extend my appreciation and give a heartfelt thank you for being loyal members of my team and great friends.

contents

Techniques A to Z

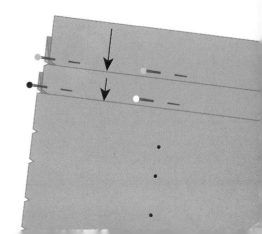

INTRODUCTION *from* NANCY

My first job after college was teaching sewing at a Minnesota Fabrics store in Chicago. Setting up twenty folding chairs in the middle of the store fifteen minutes prior to the demonstration constituted my first classroom. Since then, I've taught in almost every venue possible, with the TV studio being my most recognized classroom.

During the past thirty-five years, I've tweaked and personalized many of the common techniques. Many of these methods have been published in other books of mine, but they've never been gathered together in an A-to-Z reference. My hope is that you'll enjoy this quick reference and that these techniques will fine-tune your sewing and quilting skills.

Stitch on a small scrap of folded fabric, or anchor cloth, to secure your stitches before sailing through the stitching of your project. Just a small stitching anchor solves a multitude of stitching problems! An anchor cloth prevents the fabric from being drawn down into the bed of the sewing machine and helps heavy fabric feed freely into the machine.

A

1 Fold a scrap of fabric 2 or 3 times to form an anchor cloth.

2 Begin stitching on the anchor cloth.

It's sometimes easiest to begin stitching in the middle of the cloth. Kiss the fabric next to the edge of the anchor cloth and continue stitching.

3 After the seam is completed, clip away the anchor cloth.

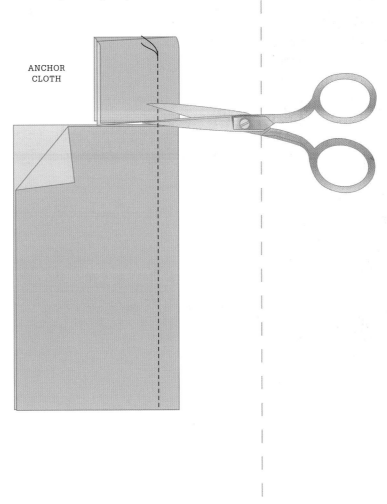

ANCHOR
CLOTH

A

A satin stitch is the most basic appliqué stitch and can be done on any machine that has an adjustable zigzag stitch. The stitches are formed so close together that they take on a satin appearance. Satin stitch appliqué eliminates the need to turn under the edges of the appliqué to keep it from fraying, plus it gives the project an enhanced appearance, especially when specialty threads are used for the stitching.

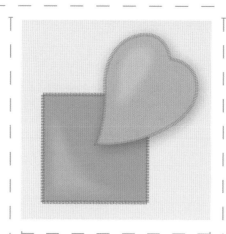

NOTE *from* NANCY

The completed appliqués will be mirror images of the tracing. Patterns that are already mirror images so they appear correctly on the completed project are the easiest to work with. If they are not already mirrored, trace the wrong side of the patterns over a light box.

1 Prepare the appliqués.

- Trace the appliqué patterns onto the paper side of paper-backed fusible web.

- Roughly cut out the designs, leaving ⅛"– ¼" (3mm–6mm) along the outer edges.

PAPER SIDE
OF FUSIBLE
WEB

- Press the paper-backed fusible web onto the wrong side of the fabric. Interface light-colored or sheer fabrics to prevent the fabric under the appliqué from showing through.

- Cut out the appliqués following the traced outlines.

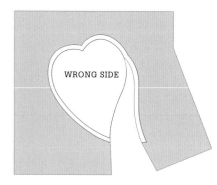

WRONG SIDE

- Remove the paper backing. To make it easier to remove the backing, lightly score the paper with a pin. Doing so provides an edge that simplifies removal.

WRONG SIDE

2 Position and fuse the appliqués on the base fabric, web-side down.

- Position background appliqués first on the base fabric; then position the foreground appliqués.

- Cover the appliqués with an appliqué pressing cloth or sheet, and fuse them in place.

PRESSING SHEET

3 Set up the machine for appliqué.

- Choose an embroidery needle, size 75. An embroidery needle has a long, wide eye to provide room for thread to pass through the needle.

- Choose a 30–40 wt. rayon, cotton or polyester thread, depending on the project fabric. Rayon and polyester embroidery threads provide a more lustrous sheen than cotton.

- Choose a lightweight bobbin thread. A lighter thread helps keep the bobbin stitching from showing on the right side of the fabric.

- Choose an open toe or embroidery presser foot. The grooved section on the underside of the foot allows stitches to easily flow through the machine, and the open area at the front of the foot allows you to more readily see where you're stitching.

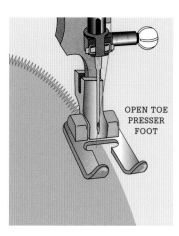

OPEN TOE PRESSER FOOT

4 Adjust the machine settings for satin stitching.

- Set stitch to zigzag.

- Set the stitch width to about 2.5mm.

- Set the stitch length to about 0.5mm–0.8mm.

- Reduce the upper tension by about two numbers or settings to keep the bobbin thread on the underside of the fabric. Check your owner's manual for recommendations for your machine.

- The feed dogs should remain in a raised position.

continued on next page >

NOTE *from* NANCY

I am often asked what the difference is between a press cloth and sheet. The cloth, since it is fabric, can be dampened prior to pressing, which provides extra moisture to your fabric. The sheet is more transparent since it is made of Teflon. You can easily see through the sheet to make certain that the appliqués are in the correct place. The sheet also helps keep your iron and pressing surface clean from stabilizer residues, starches and fusible webbing.

5 Stitch the appliqués.

- Back the appliqué with a tear-away or cut-away stabilizer suited for the fabric and project. Stabilizer prevents stitches from tunneling and helps to ensure professional results.

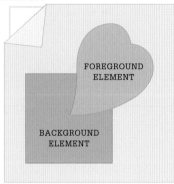

- Always test stitching on a scrap before stitching on the project.

- Lock stitches at the beginning of the stitching.

- Stitch background elements first; then stitch foreground.

- One edge of the zigzag should fall on the appliqué; the other should fall just past the raw edge of the design.

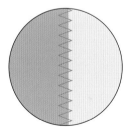

Stitching Outer Corners

- Satin stitch to the corner, with the final stitch exactly at the corner.

- Stop with the needle in the right position with the needle down in the fabric.

- Raise the presser foot and pivot the fabric so the next edge of the appliqué is in line with the needle.

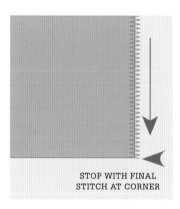

- Lower the presser foot. Give the fabric a little nudge with your hand as you stitch over the previous stitching to help the fabric advance. Continue stitching.

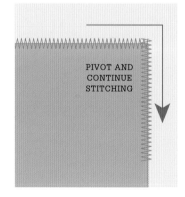

Stitching Inner Corners (as on a heart)

- Begin stitching inside the heart, about ¼" (6mm) from the edge.

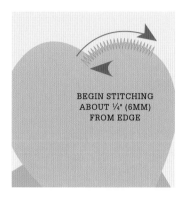

- When you approach the starting point, sew several additional stitches, overstitching the corner.

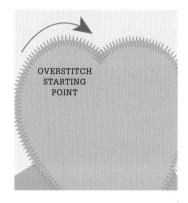

Stitching Conventional Inner Corners

- Stitch to the corner; then continue stitching three or four stitches (the width of the zigzag) past the corner.

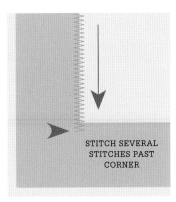

STITCH SEVERAL STITCHES PAST CORNER

- Stop with the needle in the left position, with the needle down in the fabric. Raise the presser foot and pivot the fabric so the next edge of the appliqué is in line with the needle.

- Lower the presser foot and continue to stitch.

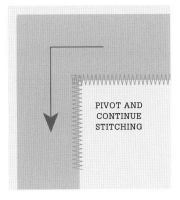

PIVOT AND CONTINUE STITCHING

Stitching Curves

- Use your left hand to lightly anchor the fabric to the sewing machine bed and gently turn the fabric as you stitch.

- On sharp curves, you may need to periodically stop and reposition the fabric to obtain a smooth curve. For **outward** curves, stop with the needle down in the **right** position. Raise the presser foot, pivot slightly, lower the foot and continue stitching. For **inward** curves, stop with the needle in the **left** position.

- On pronounced curves, reduce the stitch width to get a smooth curve.

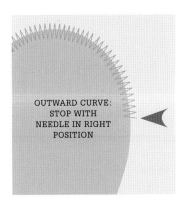

OUTWARD CURVE: STOP WITH NEEDLE IN RIGHT POSITION

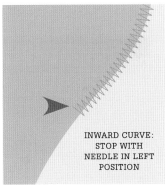

INWARD CURVE: STOP WITH NEEDLE IN LEFT POSITION

Stitching Points

- Stitch the first side of the appliqué. As you approach the point, gradually decrease the stitch width. Sew two or three stitches; reduce the stitch width to 2.0. Sew two or three more stitches; reduce width to 1.5. Repeat, tapering to a point and stopping with the needle down.

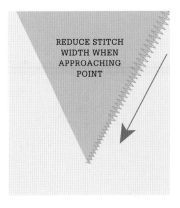

REDUCE STITCH WIDTH WHEN APPROACHING POINT

- Raise the presser foot. Pivot. Lower the foot and continue sewing, gradually increasing the stitch width to the normal 2.5 setting.

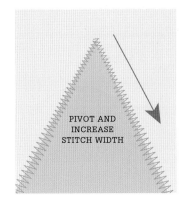

PIVOT AND INCREASE STITCH WIDTH

Realistic inner details make appliqués more artistic and full of character. Transfer inner appliqué markings with ease using my favorite technique.

1 Prepare, fuse and stitch the appliqué.

- Prepare the appliqué as for the satin stitched appliqué, tracing both the appliqué outline and any inner details onto the paper side of paper-backed fusible web (page 8).

- Press the web to the wrong side of the fabric and cut out the appliqué following the traced outline.

- Carefully remove the paper backing. Try to avoid tearing the backing—it will be used to transfer the inner markings to the appliqué.

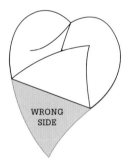

- Position and fuse the appliqué to the base fabric. Satin stitch around the outer edges, as for satin-stitched appliqué (pages 9–11).

2 Transfer the inner details using the paper backing as a guide.

- Highlight the inner details on the paper backing using a dark marker. Because the finished appliqué is a mirror image of the tracing, this makes it easier to see the markings when transferring them.

- Flip over the paper; position and pin it in place over the appliqué.

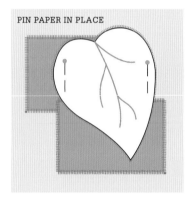
PIN PAPER IN PLACE

- Adjust the machine for a straight stitch with a short 0.6mm–0.7mm stitch length. Stitch over the traced detail lines. The short stitch length perforates the paper making it easy to remove. A short stitch length also helps produce precise details when stitching things like facial features.

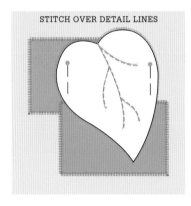
STITCH OVER DETAIL LINES

3 Stitch the details.

- Remove the paper from the appliqué piece.

- Adjust the machine for a zigzag, using a stitch length of approximately 0.7mm–0.8mm and a stitch width of approximately 1.5mm. Stitch over the straight-stitched lines, gradually decreasing the width to 0 at the point.

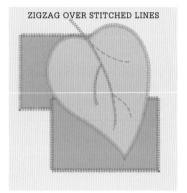
ZIGZAG OVER STITCHED LINES

Appliqué: INTERFACING TECHNIQUE

This appliqué technique is a variation of the turned-edge appliqué that quilters are so fond of. In this version there is no hand-stitching, and the curved edges have a smooth finish with minimal effort. This easy technique works best with simple shapes rather than those with significant details. Cut appliqué shapes directly from fabric, adding ⅛" (3mm) around the outer edges.

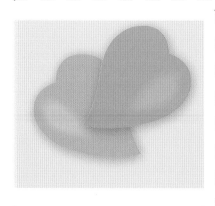

1 Position the appliqué shapes, right sides down, on a layer of lightweight interfacing.

2 Stitch completely around the appliqué just inside the cutting line, using a short stitch length.

- Using a short stitch length is crucial for getting smooth edges on the finished appliqué.

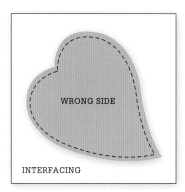

3 Cut a slit in the middle of the interfacing, taking care to avoid cutting the fabric appliqué. Press the appliqué.

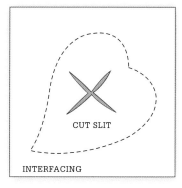

4 Complete the appliqué and stitch.

- Trim the excess outer interfacing close to the stitching line. Clip any inside corners.

- Turn the appliqué right-side-out. Roll the edges to get a crisp edge. Using a tool such as Wrights EZ Bamboo Pointer & Creaser may help achieve smooth curves.

- *Optional*: For less bulk, trim any excess interfacing inside the design to approximately ¼" (6mm) from the edge.

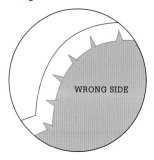

- Glue-baste the appliqués to the background.

- Stitch the appliqués in place with monofilament thread. A blanket stitch or a blind hem stitch works well for this method of appliqué. The outer edge of the stitch should follow the outer edge of the appliqué, while the zig will fall on the appliqué.

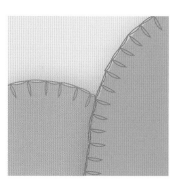

13

B

Basting is the temporary stitching that is used for marking pattern pieces, matching plaids, attaching interfacing, holding slippery fabric pieces together for stitching and more. Hand-basting, pin-basting and machine-basting are the methods traditionally used. Choose the method that is the easiest for you to accomplish and enjoy.

Pin-Basting for Fitting

- To pin-baste a garment, place pins on the right side of the garment parallel to the seamline. This allows you to move pins as the garment is being tried on.

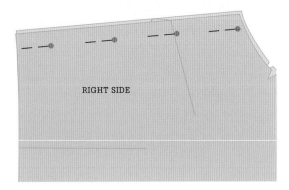

RIGHT SIDE

Machine-Basting

- Machine-baste sturdy fabrics that aren't slippery and won't show needle marks. Set your sewing machine for the longest stitch and loosen the upper tension slightly for easier removal. Or clip the top stitches at intervals; then pull on the bottom thread to remove the stitches.

- Many machines have a special extra-long basting stitch that is very easy to remove. This specialty stitch is especially nice for quilting to temporarily hold fabric layers together. Check your manual to see if this stitch is available on your machine.

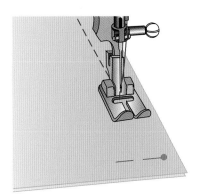

Hand-Basting

- Use an **even** basting stitch for long seams that are subject to strain and for areas such as set-in sleeves that demand close control. Space the stitches evenly, about ¼" (6mm) long and ¼" (6mm) apart. Start and stop stitching with a backstitch rather than a knot.

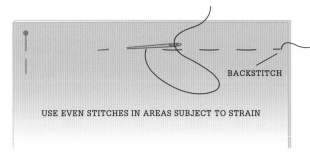

BACKSTITCH

USE EVEN STITCHES IN AREAS SUBJECT TO STRAIN

- Use an **uneven** basting stitch to hold fabric together at seams and edges that are not subject to strain, such as in a hem. Take a long stitch on top and a short stitch through the fabric. Start and stop stitching with a backstitch rather than a knot.

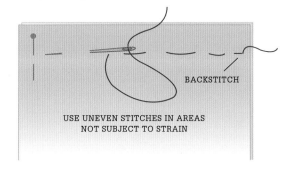

BACKSTITCH

USE UNEVEN STITCHES IN AREAS
NOT SUBJECT TO STRAIN

I like to make fabric loops for slacks and purses, as ties and hangers, and even as a unique coordinating trim. Make them quickly by using my easy-fold technique or by using a specialty belt loop binder attachment for a cover stitch serger.

B

Easy-Fold Fabric Loops

1 Cut 1½"–2" (38mm–51mm) crosswise fabric strips the length needed.

2 Fold and press the strips in half lengthwise, wrong sides together.

3 Open the fold and align the lengthwise edges with the fold mark. Press.

4 Fold the strip in half lengthwise. Then edgestitch to hide and secure the raw edges.

Cover Stitch Fabric Loops

- Check your serger owner's manual to see if a belt loop binder attachment is available for your machine.

- Follow the instructions for your specific serger to make these belt loops using a triple cover stitch. They're just like the ones shown on ready-to-wear garments!

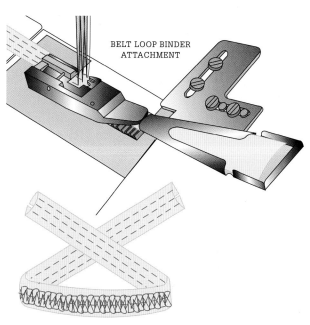

BELT LOOP BINDER
ATTACHMENT

TRIPLE COVER STITCHED
FABRIC LOOPS

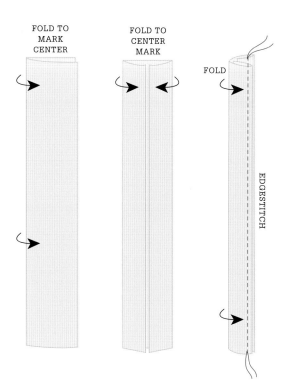

FOLD TO
MARK
CENTER

FOLD TO
CENTER
MARK

FOLD

EDGESTITCH

B

Thread loops are perfect for holding a belt on a fitted dress, as button loops, as corded buttonholes and even for making tassels. Make thread loops quickly using your conventional machine or a chain stitch serger.

Conventional Thread Loops

1 Zigzag over six strands of thread while holding them taut.

2 Use a stitch width of 4 and a stitch length of 1.

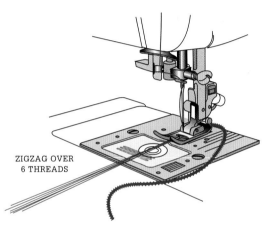

ZIGZAG OVER
6 THREADS

Serger Thread Loops

1 Adjust your serger for a center needle chain stitch. (Check your serger manual to make sure your machine is capable of doing a chain stitch.)

2 Disengage the blade and upper looper. Attach the sewing table.

3 Use a decorative thread in the chain looper if desired.

4 Fold a piece of cotton fabric in half and position it under the needle as an anchor cloth (page 7). On many chain stitch sergers, it is necessary to start a chain stitch on an anchor cloth.

5 Serge beyond the fabric to form a thread chain the desired length.

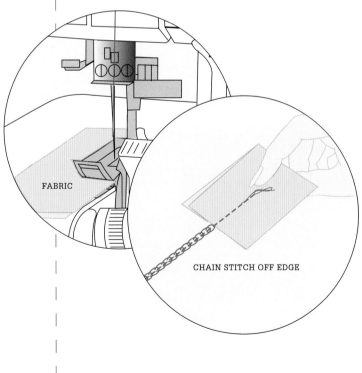

FABRIC

CHAIN STITCH OFF EDGE

Bias is the direction of fabric that has the most stretch. True bias is located in a 45-degree angle between the length and the width of the fabric. Bias-cut fabric or trim can be manipulated with ease around curved areas of garments and used to form shapely designs.

B

Bias Basics

- The construction of woven fabric is made up of two sets of yarns: lengthwise yarns and crosswise yarns. Lengthwise yarns, or warp yarns, run parallel to the selvage edges and have a very small amount of stretch. Crosswise yarns, or weft yarns, are woven across the fabric from selvage to selvage at right angles to the lengthwise yarns. Crosswise yarns tend to stretch more than lengthwise yarns.

- Measure from the corner of the fabric the same distance both along the selvage and the crossgrain. Draw a line connecting those two points to find the true bias or the highest degree of stretch in the fabric.

- The bias of a woven fabric stretches, even if the fabric is very stable. That bias stretch allows bias trim to be molded and shaped around curves, and it can be used to finish curved garment edges, such as armholes and necklines.

- Create custom bias strips or bias tape from the woven fabric of your choice.

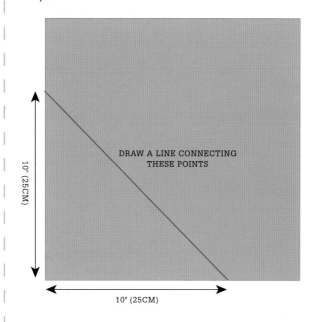

10" (25CM)

DRAW A LINE CONNECTING
THESE POINTS

10" (25CM)

Bias Strips

1 Cut bias strips.

- Align the 45-degree angle of a quilting ruler along the fabric selvage and cut the angle with a rotary cutter. Or form a true bias (page 17), and cut along the line.

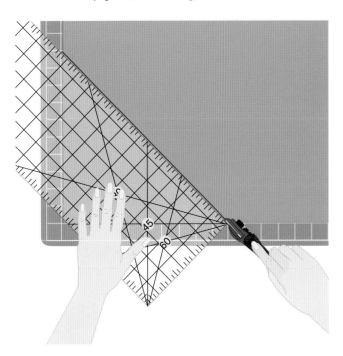

- Cut ½" (13mm) strips along the bias edge.

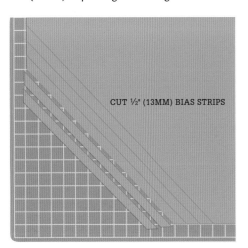

CUT ½" (13MM) BIAS STRIPS

2 Join the bias strips.

- Place the short ends of two strips right sides together at a 90-degree angle, offsetting the ends by approximately ¼" (6mm). Small triangles of fabric will extend on each edge.

- Mark a diagonal line from corner to corner. Using a short stitch length, stitch along the line.

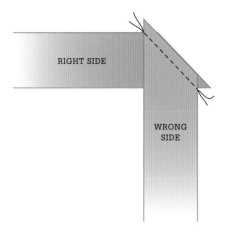

RIGHT SIDE

WRONG SIDE

- Press the seam open. If desired, trim the triangle extensions.

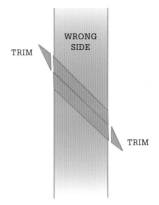

WRONG SIDE

TRIM

TRIM

- Join additional strips to obtain the necessary length of bias strips.

Bias Tape

1 Create ¼" (6mm) bias tape.

- Insert a ½" (13mm) bias strip, wrong side up, into the wide end of a ¼" (6mm) bias tape maker.

- Use a pin to advance the fabric through the opening slot in the bias tape maker. Press the fabric as it comes through the tool.

- When nearing a seam, press the seam allowances away from the bias tape maker. As the seam goes through the tool, you may need to advance and press in even shorter increments to prevent the seam allowances from buckling and creating a taper with an uneven width.

NOTE *from* NANDY

When using a bias tape maker, it's important to work in small increments, advancing the fabric no more than 1" (25mm) at a time before pressing. This helps ensure that the completed tape will be smooth and of a uniform width.

2 Add fusible web to the bias tape.

- Cut scant ¼" (6mm) strips from a fusible web, such as HeatnBond Lite Iron-On Adhesive.

- Position the fusible web on the wrong side of the bias tape. Press, fusing the web to the tape.

PAPER SIDE OF FUSIBLE WEB

Fusible Bias

Use ready-made fusible bias, such as Quick Bias, as an easy alternative to making your own bias with fusible web.

Fusible bias is a prefolded, preshrunk ¼" (6mm) bias tape with finished edges and a fusible backing. It is available in a variety of solid and rainbow colors, as well as metallics. It is used mainly for trim on garments and quilts and for a decorative effect in stained glass appliqué.

- Remove the paper from the adhesive side of the fusible bias.

- Position the bias with the fusible side down on the fabric. Press into position.

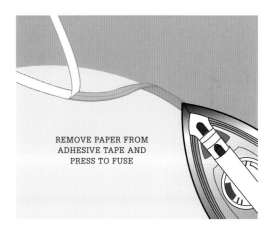

REMOVE PAPER FROM
ADHESIVE TAPE AND
PRESS TO FUSE

NOTE *from* NANDY

Save time by using a fusible bias tape maker. It guides the fabric strip and fusible tape through separate openings. It folds the fabric strip and positions the paper-backed fusible strip so that when they come out the tip, they are aligned and ready to be pressed together.

B

Add a finishing touch to your quilts, wall hangings, home décor and wearable art when you cover the raw edges with binding. The techniques for double- and single-fold binding are easy, and they complete your project with a band of color.

Double-Fold Binding

1 Cut 2½" (6cm) crosswise strips of binding, joining the strips as needed for extra length. Join the short ends of the strips with diagonal seams to reduce bulk when the binding is folded to the wrong side.

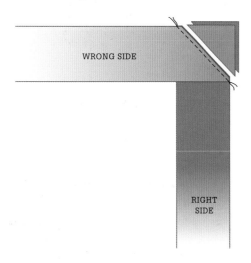

WRONG SIDE

RIGHT SIDE

2 Cut one end of the strip at a 45-degree angle. Fold in ¼" (6mm) at the angled end of the binding. (*Optional*: Press a ¼" [6mm] strip of paper-backed fusible web on top of the folded-under edge.) Fold the binding in half with wrong sides together, matching the lengthwise edges. Press. (Leave paper in place.)

FUSIBLE WEB

WRONG SIDE

FOLD

NOTE *from* NANCY

Use bias binding strips to bind large curved areas. Find more information about bias strips on page 18.

3 Mark the quilt top ¼" (6mm) from each corner.

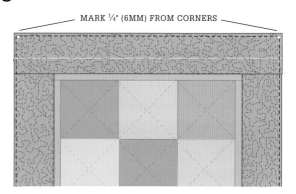

MARK ¼" (6MM) FROM CORNERS

4 Place the raw edges of the binding right sides together with the quilt top, beginning at the center of one edge of the quilt. Stitch the binding to the quilt top with a ¼" (6mm) seam, starting stitches about 4" (10cm) from the end of the binding. Stop stitching at the marked point. Lock stitches by stitching in place or stitching in reverse.

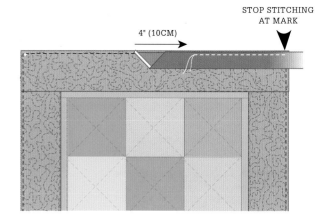

STOP STITCHING AT MARK

4" (10CM)

5 Fold the binding up at a 45-degree angle, aligning the cut edges of the binding with the cut edge of the quilt.

6 Fold the binding down, matching the binding fold to the top edge of the quilt, and matching the binding cut edges to the quilt side edges. Starting at the marked point, stitch a ¼" (6mm) seam down the side. Repeat at the remaining corners.

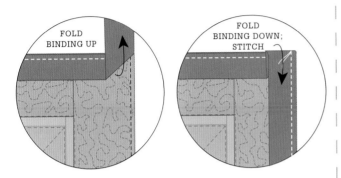

7 When the binding reaches the starting point, overlap the binding and trim the excess. If a strip of paper-backed fusible web was used, remove the paper backing from the folded-under end of the binding.

INSERT BINDING END; STITCH REMAINDER OF SEAM

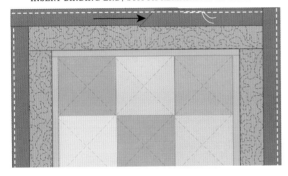

8 Fold and press the binding away from the quilt.

9 Fold the binding to the wrong side, covering the stitching line and tucking in the corners to form miters. Hand-stitch the folded edges of the binding to the quilt backing, or stitch in the ditch, sewing in the well of the seam.

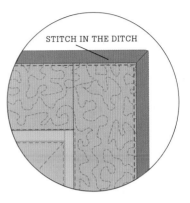

Single-Fold Binding

1 Cut 1½" (4cm) crosswise strips.

2 Stitch the binding to the quilt or wearable art by following steps 4–9 as detailed in *Double-Fold Binding* (pages 20–21).

3 Fold the cut edge of the binding under ¼" (6mm), and fold the binding to the back of the quilt or garment. Stitch the binding down by hand with a single thread that matches the binding color.

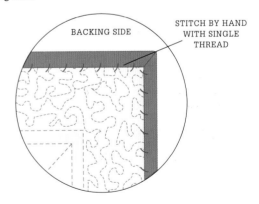

NOTE *from* NANCY

Use single-fold binding for midweight to heavy-weight fabrics, such as those used in wearable art.

B

Getting hand-stitched blanket stitches perfectly spaced once required tedious, time-consuming measuring. Here's a clever way to add uniform blanket stitching to an edge with absolutely no measuring involved: Turn that task over to your sewing machine!

1 Adjust the sewing machine.

- Set the machine for a long blind hem stitch.

- Loosen the top tension by two numbers or notches.

- Stitch an even distance from the edge, approximately ¼"–½" (6mm–13mm) from the edge.

NOTE *from* NANCY

Some of my favorite threads to use for blanket stitching include DMC floss or Madeira Silk Embroidery Floss. The size of the hand sewing needle depends upon the number of strands of floss selected. Select a hand sewing needle that will accommodate the thickness of the floss.

2 Hand-stitch a blanket stitch by bringing the needle through the fabric at each zig of the blind hem stitch.

- Insert the needle from the back at point **A**.

- Insert the needle at point **B**, and bring it out again at point **C** at the edge of the fabric. Make sure the thread or yarn is under the point of the needle as shown.

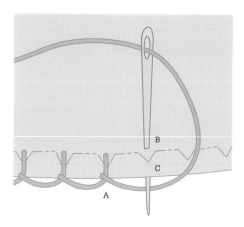

- Repeat, working from left to right and always keeping the needle over the yarn.

- Remove the basting stitches after the hand-stitching is completed.

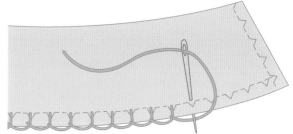

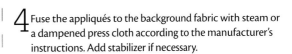

B

Small, even blanket stitches can be achieved effectively by using your sewing machine with a few minor adjustments. Machine blanket stitching is perfect for appliqué when you want a unique stitch that resembles folk art appliqué!

1 Adjust the sewing machine.

- Set the machine for a blanket stitch with a stitch width of 2.0mm–4.0mm and a length of approximately 2.5mm.

- Test the settings by stitching on a scrap of fabric, and adjust if necessary.

2 Trace the appliqués on paper-backed fusible web. Roughly cut out the appliqués leaving ¼" (6mm) around the outer edges.

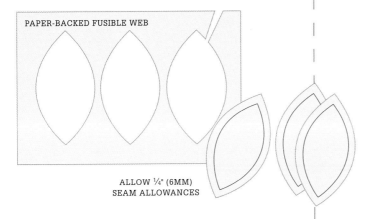

PAPER-BACKED FUSIBLE WEB

ALLOW ¼" (6MM)
SEAM ALLOWANCES

3 Apply the paper-backed fusible web appliqués to the wrong side of the fabrics; press with a dry iron to secure. Cut out the appliqués along the traced lines. Remove the paper backing.

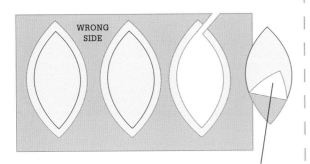

WRONG
SIDE

REMOVE PAPER
BACKING

4 Fuse the appliqués to the background fabric with steam or a dampened press cloth according to the manufacturer's instructions. Add stabilizer if necessary.

5 Machine-stitch around each appliqué using the blanket stitch. The straight stitch should follow the edge of the appliqué, with the zig falling within the appliqué.

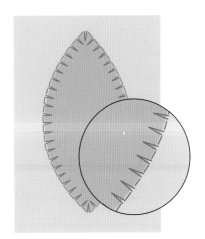

NOTE *from* NANCY

Some paper-backed fusible web products have a tacky web that allows you to position pieces temporarily before fusing them in place. This helps you audition the placement of the appliqués before fusing them permanently.

B

The main goal in blind hemming is for the stitches to be practically invisible. It's important to allow a little slack in the thread to prevent puckers.

1 Press up the hem.

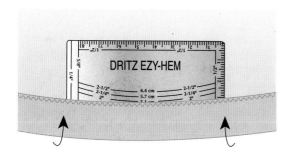

NOTE *from* NANCY

I like to use a metal hem gauge when pressing a hem so I can press and measure in one easy step. A hem gauge has both curved and straight edges to accommodate straight or curved hems.

2 Fold back the main fabric, exposing ¼" (6mm) of the hem allowance.

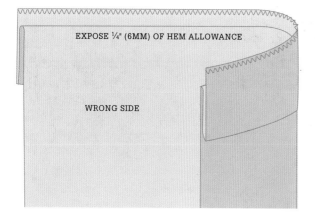

EXPOSE ¼" (6MM) OF HEM ALLOWANCE

WRONG SIDE

3 Anchor the thread in the hem allowance by taking two or more stitches on top of each other.

4 Stitch right to left in the fold of the fabric, picking up just a few threads of fabric with each stitch.

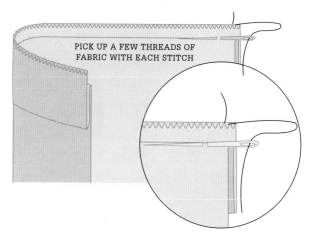

PICK UP A FEW THREADS OF FABRIC WITH EACH STITCH

5 Stitch from right to left in the hem allowance, approximately ½" (13mm) from the stitching in the fold. The stitch resembles an elongated X shape, which builds in a slight amount of stretch so the hem doesn't pull and pucker.

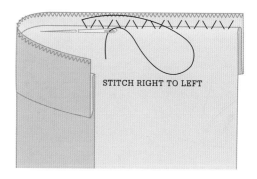

STITCH RIGHT TO LEFT

It's always faster to hem by machine rather than by hand. The important step is to always test the stitch to make certain that the width of the stitch isn't set too wide.

1 Press the hem following steps 1–2 of *Blind Hemming: Hand* (page 24).

2 Set up the machine for a blind hem stitch as detailed in your owner's manual.

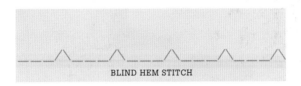

BLIND HEM STITCH

3 Attach a blind hem foot with a center guide.

4 Stitch with the fold of the fabric along the guide on the blind hem foot.

• Test to make sure the stitch is catching the fold of the fabric. If the stitch shows too much on the right side or doesn't stitch into the fold, lengthen or shorten the stitch width to correct the problem.

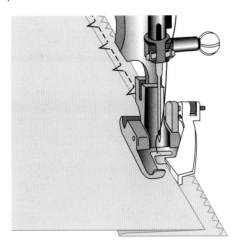

NOTE *from* NANCY

Use monofilament thread in the needle to assure that the hem is invisible.

B

Perfectly sized buttonholes are a must for garments that look nice and are securely fastened. Learn buttonhole basics to accurately measure, mark, stitch and open buttonholes. If you anticipate that your buttonhole will get a lot of wear, consider making a corded buttonhole. It's a great buttonhole reinforcement!

Buttonhole Basics

1 Determine the correct length of the buttonhole.

- Use tape to measure proper buttonhole length.
  - Place a length of tape, such as Sewer's Fix-It Tape, over the button. Start at the lower edge, extend the tape across the top, and stop at the opposite lower edge to allow for both the length and width of the button.
  - Mark both lower edges of the button on the tape.

MARK LOWER EDGES OF BUTTONS

  - Remove the tape from the button. Straighten the tape and extend the marks. Save the tape to use as a guideline when sewing the buttonhole. Stitch the buttonhole next to, but not through, the tape.

EXTEND MARKS

2 Use a sliding buttonhole foot.

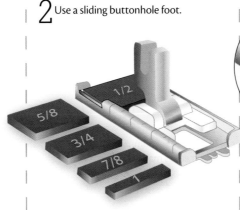

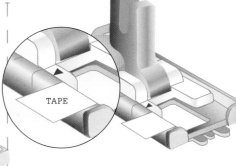

- Place the button in the sliding tray at the back of the foot so it's even with the edge of the tray.
- Slide the tray to meet the button.

- Note the position of the arrow at the front of the foot. Grids are marked on the foot in ¼" (6mm) increments. Place a piece of tape half a marking (⅛" [3mm]) lower than the arrow position to allow for the depth of the button. This identifies the position where the buttonhole should stop.
- Remove the button.

NOTE *from* NANCY

Take a careful look at the back of the buttonhole foot. When you place a button in the tray and slide the tray back, part of the button can extend into the opening at the end of the foot. This could make your finished buttonhole too small. To compensate, lengthen the buttonhole by ⅛" (3mm). Or as an alternative, carefully place the button so it does not extend beyond the tray.

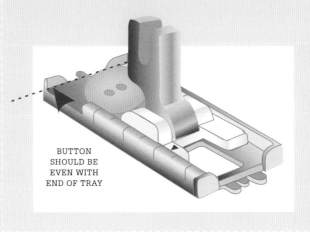

BUTTON SHOULD BE EVEN WITH END OF TRAY

3 Select a stabilizer.

- Use lightweight tear-away stabilizer under woven fabrics.

- Use water-soluble stabilizer both on top of and under knit fabrics.

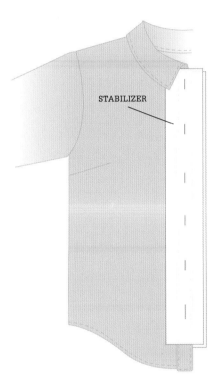

STABILIZER

4 Set up the machine.

- Thread the top and bobbin of the machine with matching thread. Since buttonholes may be both functional and decorative, consider using rayon embroidery thread.

- Loosen the tension by two notches or numbers.

- Attach a buttonhole foot.

- Adjust the stitch length according to fabric type. Begin with the settings recommended in your owner's manual.

5 Stitch a trial buttonhole following the instructions in your sewing machine owner's manual.

- Duplicate the fabric, interfacing and grainline in your sample because the finished buttonhole may be slightly different if these factors vary.

6 Use your favorite method for opening a buttonhole. I like to use a buttonhole cutter and block.

- Place the buttonhole over the block, positioning the cutter blade in the center of the buttonhole. Cut.

- If the buttonhole is smaller than the blade, place half the buttonhole over the block and cut. Repeat on the uncut half.

- If the buttonhole is larger than the blade, open part of the buttonhole; then repeat, opening the remainder of the buttonhole.

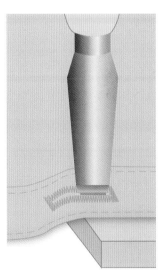

continued on next page >

7 Mark the buttonhole spacing on the project.

- Decide whether the buttonhole will be horizontal or vertical.

  - Use horizontal buttonholes for closely fitting garments or at points of strain, like waistbands. End horizontal buttonholes ⅛" (3mm) beyond the center front or back.

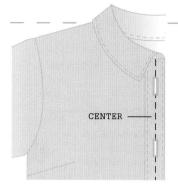

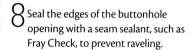

CENTER

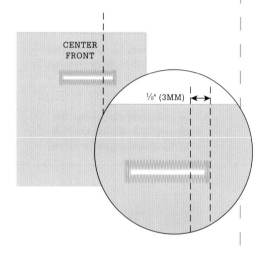

CENTER FRONT

⅛" (3MM)

- Use vertical buttonholes on shirt plackets where centering the buttonhole would be important. Also use them on knit fabrics, since the crosswise stretch of the fabric may cause a horizontal buttonhole to gape. Position vertical buttonholes on the centerline.

- Mark the actual buttonhole positions in one of these ways:

  - Use a fabric marking pen or pencil. This technique is a good choice when using the sliding buttonhole foot or another method where the length of the buttonhole is measured by the foot.

  - Mark beginning and ending points on Sewer's Fix-It Tape. Place the tape slightly to the side of or below the buttonhole to prevent stitching through the tape.

  - Use Space Tape. This see-through, pressure-sensitive tape is printed with horizontal and vertical markings, in sizes ranging from ½"–1" (13mm–25mm). Corresponding buttonholes are spaced 3½" (9cm) apart, the standard buttonhole spacing. The tape acts as a stabilizer as well as a guideline. Stitch through the tape, and then carefully remove the excess tape. Save unused sections on wax paper to use at another time.

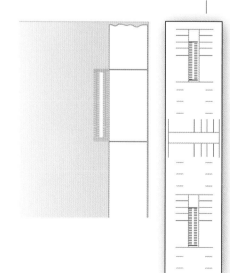

8 Seal the edges of the buttonhole opening with a seam sealant, such as Fray Check, to prevent raveling.

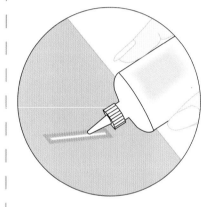

Corded Buttonholes

1 Use purchased cording, or make your own cording using this easy technique.

- Use a conventional presser foot.

- Pull the top and bobbin threads together, allowing about 7" (18cm) per buttonhole.

- Fold the thread back on itself, pulling out a total of about six strands of thread. Twist the strands together and place under the presser foot.

- Hold threads in front and back of the machine as you zigzag over them using a 2.0mm–2.5mm stitch length.

2 Cut the cording into approximately 7" (18cm) lengths.

3 Attach a buttonhole foot. Loop the cording section around the toe at the back of the foot, and bring the cording under and to the front of the foot, crossing the cords in the three-pronged toe.

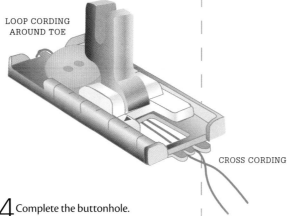

LOOP CORDING AROUND TOE

CROSS CORDING

4 Complete the buttonhole.

- Stitch the buttonhole over the cording.

- Pull the cut ends of the cording until the loop in the back of the buttonhole disappears.

- Thread the cut ends through a large-eyed needle and pull to the wrong side of the fabric. Knot the cords together and trim.

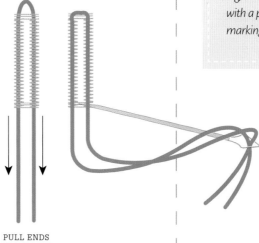

PULL ENDS OF CORDING

NOTE *from* NANCY

If the interfacing shows through the buttonhole opening, color the fabric edges with a permanent fabric marking pen.

B

Save time sewing buttons by using your sewing machine, and create beautiful thread shanks with ease. Some sewing machines have a special stitch setting and foot for sewing on buttons, but if yours doesn't, simply use a fringe foot and zigzag stitch.

1 Attach a fringe foot. The center bar of the fringe foot creates the button shank.

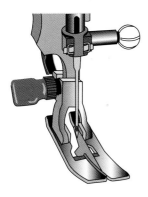

NOTE *from* NANCY

STIR STICK

If you don't have access to a fringe foot, you can improvise by using a coffee stir stick or toothpick taped to your regular presser foot. Sewing over the stick is much like sewing over the center bar on the fringe foot to give your button a nice shank. It's rather unconventional looking and not as durable, but it works!

2 Tape the button to the project using transparent tape or Sewer's Fix-It Tape.

- Position the tape so the stitching doesn't pierce the tape, if possible.

- Turn the flywheel by hand to ensure the needle bar clears the foot's center bar and the stitching is aligned with the openings in the button.

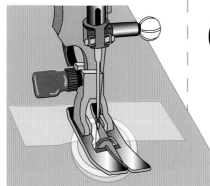

3 Zigzag five or six stitches in place using a length of 0 and a stitch width of approximately 2.0mm.

4 Raise the presser foot and remove the stitching from the center bar by gently slipping the stitches off the foot. Cut the threads, leaving long thread tails.

5 Separate the button and the project so the thread shank floats between the two.

6 Thread a needle with the thread tails. Draw the thread tails to the center, between the button and the fabric.

7 Wrap the thread tails around the thread shank. Tie the threads, or bring the tails to the underside of the fabric and tie off.

8 Apply a drop of seam sealant, such as Fray Check or Fray Block, to the shank. This reinforces the shank and provides added security.

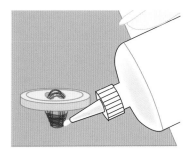

Casings are generally made to enclose ribbon, self-fabric ties or elastic to gather up fabric for fitting, closing or decorating an area. You'll find this technique for an elastic casing to be the simplest one ever!

1 Form the casing.

- Zigzag or serge the casing edge.

- Turn under and prepress the casing on each cut piece using a hem gauge for accuracy. Prepressing this edge makes it easier to turn and stitch the casing later.

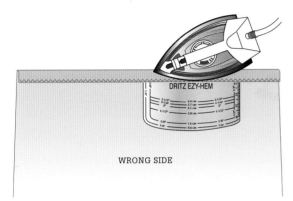

WRONG SIDE

- Stitch the side and/or center seams, leaving one of the seams unstitched from the foldline to the cut edge of the casing. (If there is a center back seam, that's a good place for the opening.)

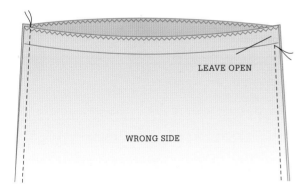

LEAVE OPEN

WRONG SIDE

- Press the seams flat; then press the seams open.

- Trim away half the width of the seam between the casing foldline and the cut edge to reduce bulk.

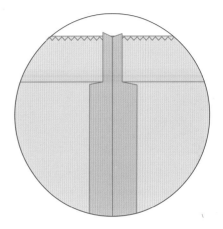

- Machine baste each seam allowance to the garment about 3" (8cm) from the upper edge. This prevents the elastic from getting caught under the seam when it is inserted.

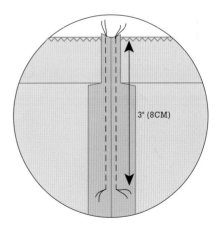

3" (8CM)

- Fold the casing to the wrong side along the prepressed casing line. Pin the casing to the garment/project. Check to ensure that the unstitched edges of the final seam meet at the seamline.

continued on next page >

- Stitch around the lower edge of the casing. Use a stitching guide so the stitching is a uniform distance from the edge. Also stitch around the top of the casing, approximately ⅛" (3mm) from the folded edge. The distance between the two lines of stitching must be slightly greater than the width of the elastic.

WRONG SIDE

2 Measure and insert the elastic.

- Cut the elastic about 2" (5cm) smaller than the finished measurement desired.

- Center a 2" (5cm) square of firmly woven fabric under one cut edge of the elastic. Securely zigzag the elastic to the fabric.

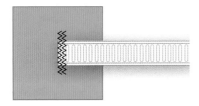

- Attach an elastic guide or bodkin to the unstitched end of the elastic. Thread the elastic through the opening in the seam. The fabric square will help stop the free end of the elastic from being drawn into the seam opening.

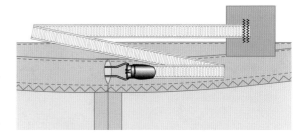

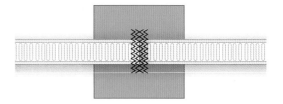

- Kiss the other end of the elastic against the first end. Zigzag through the elastic and fabric several times.

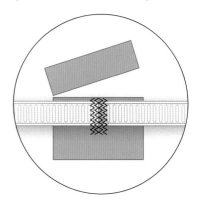

- Trim away excess fabric that extends beyond the elastic.

- Distribute fullness evenly around the casing. Remove the basting stitches.

The process of stitching multiple patchwork blocks, triangles or strata pieces without cutting the threads between the units is known as chain stitching. It's a great time-saving technique.

C

1 Set the machine for a short stitch length, 12–15 stitches per inch.

2 Align the blocks, triangles or strips of fabric with right sides together. Stitch a seam as the pattern indicates.

3 At the end of the first seam, do not raise the presser foot or cut the threads.

4 Kiss the second set of blocks, triangles or strips to the first and continue sewing, chain stitching the sections together.

5 Clip the threads between the sections after chain stitching all like pieces.

KISS STRIPS AND CHAIN TOGETHER

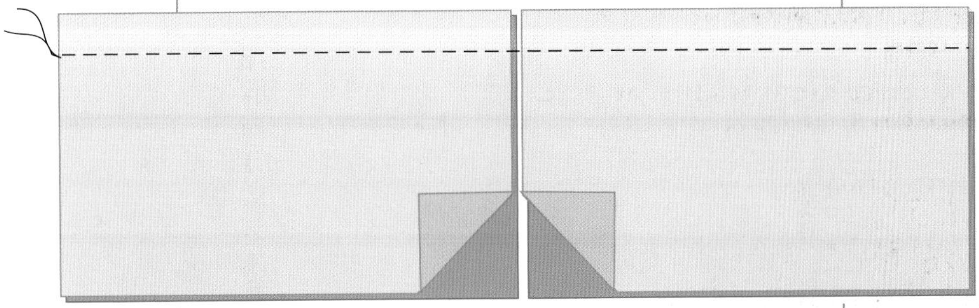

NOTE *from* NANCY

Serger chain stitching is a specific type of stitch. Refer to page 104 for more information.

C

Mark and cut circles with ease using one of the many cutters and rulers on the market, or use your imagination and various round household items. I use two simple methods to make most of the circles for my sewing and quilting projects.

1 Various size round plates work well for marking designs and quilting templates. Cups, saucers and jar or bottle tops serve well for marking yo-yos and appliqué templates.

2 A yardstick compass may be a good investment for extra-large circles (up to 72" [183cm] diameter) and those that need to be a specific size.

- Attach the yardstick compass to a yardstick.

- Place the pointed end of the yardstick compass at the 0" (0mm) marking and the pencil point at the measurement that is half of the diameter. (For example: Place the pencil point at the 21" [53cm] marking for a circle with a 42" [107cm] diameter.)

- Draw the circle pattern on paper for your project.

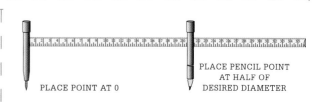

PLACE POINT AT 0

PLACE PENCIL POINT AT HALF OF DESIRED DIAMETER

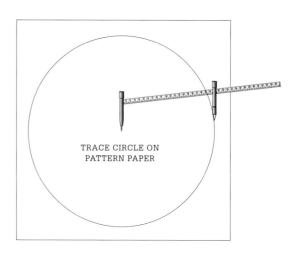

TRACE CIRCLE ON PATTERN PAPER

C

Clipping is a very important part of sewing. Curved areas of a garment like necklines and other curved seams just won't curve if they aren't clipped! Those little nips to the seamline on inner curves allow a little flexibility. Just be careful not to clip past the seamline!

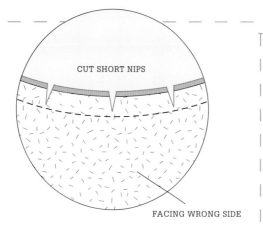

CUT SHORT NIPS

FACING WRONG SIDE

If a seam has a sharp or pronounced curve, you may need to clip the seam to make it lie flat. Clipping may be necessary on princess-style seams and/or facings. Cut short nips perpendicular to the seamline.

Streamline your pattern cutting time whether you use a pair of shears or a rotary cutter. One of my favorite cutting surfaces is a ping-pong table! If using a rotary cutter, invest in a large cutting mat that can be positioned underneath your fabric before cutting.

C

Cutting Patterns with a Shears

- Move around the fabric as you cut instead of moving the fabric toward you. You will be less likely to distort the grainline of the fabric.

- Cut along the marked pattern lines, trimming notches off as you cut for a smoother line. Notches can be marked later with short nips.

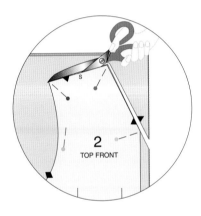

- Cut out the interfacing at the same time you cut out the rest of the project.

- Use a sharp scissors or shears, and cut with long, smooth strokes. For best results, use an 8" (20cm) dressmaker shears for cutting fabrics.

- Sharpen your sewing shears periodically to ensure clean-cut edges.

  - Use a sharpening stone, sliding the stone upward along the beveled surface of the knife edge blade, working from the shank of the blade to the tip.

  - Cut into a piece of fabric, starting at the base of the shears and cutting all the way to the tip of the shears to remove any burrs left from the sharpening process.

  - After honing, wipe the blade clean.

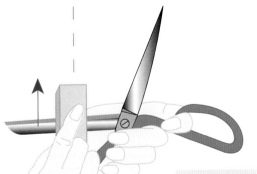

Cutting Patterns with a Rotary Cutter

1 Use a cutting mat and ruler with a rotary cutter to cut out patterns.

- Use a small 28mm rotary cutter for light- to medium-weight fabrics as it provides greater maneuverability around curves and tight corners.

- Use a large 45mm–60mm cutter for straight edges and heavier fabrics.

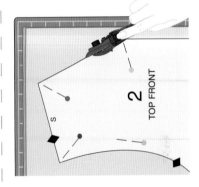

2 Use a clear gridded ruler as a guide when cutting straight lines.

NOTE *from* NANCY

To keep your sewing shears in good condition, use it only on fabric. Cutting paper dulls your sewing shears very quickly. Have a pair of paper-cutting scissors specifically for cutting craft projects and precutting paper patterns.

C

Stratas, or strips of fabric sewn together, are the basis for many patchwork designs. Rotary-cut fabric into strips, stitch the strips together and then subcut them into sections. This saves time, increases accuracy and eliminates the need for templates.

1 Prepare the fabric for cutting.

• Fold the fabric in half, meeting the selvage edges.

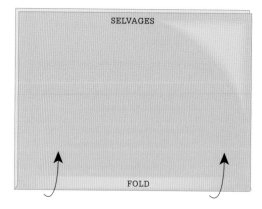

• Fold the fabric again, bringing the fold to the selvages. (There now will be four layers of fabric.)

• Place the fabric on a rotary cutting mat, aligning the fold along one of the horizontal lines at the lower edge of the mat.

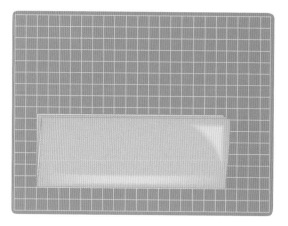

• Position a ruler on the fabric perpendicular to the fold so it forms a right angle. Straighten the fabric edge, using a rotary cutter to trim away any excess fabric.

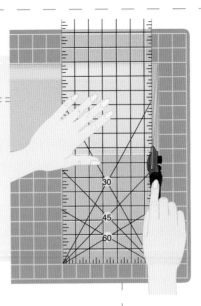

For greatest accuracy, I prefer to have the majority of the fabric to the left of the ruler when I make that first cut to straighten the edge. Firmly hold the ruler in position with your left hand, and cut with your right. Then carefully rotate the mat so the trimmed edge of the fabric is on the left before cutting the strips.

2 Cut the strips.

• Determine the strip width. The width of the strip is determined by the completed design.

• Align one of the ruler's horizontal lines with the fabric fold. Working from the straightened edge, place the line corresponding to the desired strip width along the straightened edge of the fabric.

• Cut the fabric into crosswise strips.

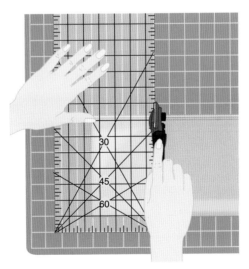

D

Do darts have you in a dither? Stitch a straight, dimple-free dart in seconds using your top thread as a stitching guide.

1 Mark the dart.

- Make short ½" (6mm) clips at the cut edges of the dart.

- Use a washable marking pencil or chalk to mark the point of the dart.

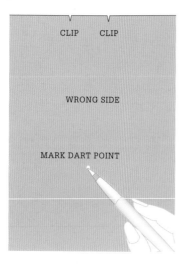

CLIP   CLIP

WRONG SIDE

MARK DART POINT

2 Fold the dart, right sides together, meeting the ¼" (6mm) clips.

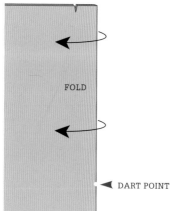

FOLD

◄ DART POINT

3 Before lowering the presser foot, pull the top thread slightly longer than the dart length. Place the fabric under the presser foot, lower the presser foot and stitch one stitch.

4 Lay the thread on top of the fabric to mark the stitching line between the nips and the dart point.

5 Set the machine to straight stitch and sew the dart, following the thread guide.

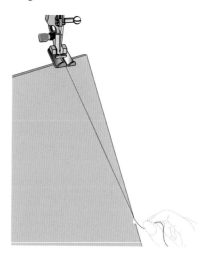

6 At the end of the dart, turn the machine's wheel by hand, just barely catching two or three stitches along the dart fold.

7 Tie the thread by chain stitching, sewing off the fabric and allowing the threads to lock together.

8 Attach the tail to the dart. Sew two or three stitches; then cut the threads.

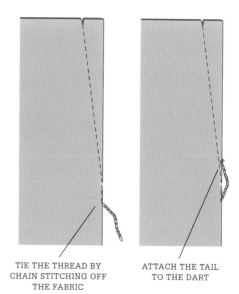

TIE THE THREAD BY
CHAIN STITCHING OFF
THE FABRIC

ATTACH THE TAIL
TO THE DART

Decorative stitches are a mainstay on most sewing machines, yet unfortunately we rarely use them. Here are a few tips on how to use decorative stitches so you'll feel confident adding a touch of artful sewing to your next project.

D

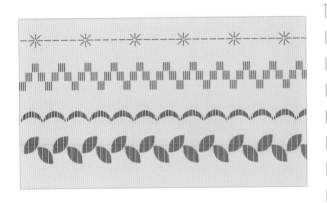

1 Insert an embroidery or open toe foot and an embroidery needle on your sewing machine.

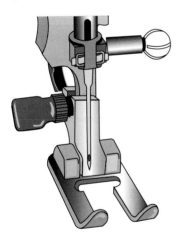

2 Thread the top of the machine with rayon, cotton or polyester embroidery thread. Use a lightweight thread such as Madeira Bobbinfil Thread or prewound bobbins in the bobbin.

- Using a lightweight bobbin thread helps keep the bobbin thread from showing on the right side of the fabric.

3 Use a stabilizer to improve stitch quality. For more information, see *Stabilizers* (pages 118–119).

4 Loosen the top tension by two numbers or notches.

- This helps draw the top thread to the underside of the fabric and keeps the bobbin thread out of view.

5 Test the stitching on a sample to determine whether the stabilizer and thread tension are appropriate.

- The bobbin thread should remain on the underside of the fabric. It should not be visible on the right side.

- The top thread should be drawn slightly to the underside so it is visible on the wrong side of the fabric.

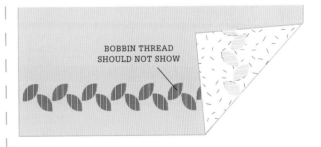

BOBBIN THREAD SHOULD NOT SHOW

D

A double needle has two needles attached to a single shaft, so on the right side of a double-needle stitched hem, you'll see two perfectly parallel rows of stitching. On the wrong side of the fabric, a single bobbin thread moves back and forth between the two needle threads and looks similar to a zigzag stitch.

Sizes

Double or twin needles are identified by the distance in millimeters between the two needles. Common double needle sizes include:

- 1.6mm needle, size 80
- 2.0mm needle, size 80
- 3.0mm needle, size 80
- 4.0mm needle, size 80
- 6.0mm needle, size 100

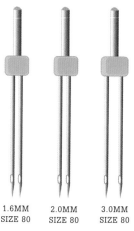

1.6MM
SIZE 80   2.0MM
SIZE 80   3.0MM
SIZE 80

4.0MM
SIZE 80   6.0MM
SIZE 100

Uses

Use narrow double needles to sew heirloom stitches. Use wider double needles for facings, hems and necklines.

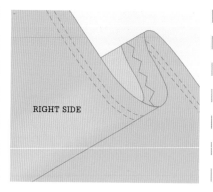

RIGHT SIDE

Double-Needle Hemming

A double-needle topstitched hem is ideal for knits, since the bobbin thread zigzags between the top threads to build in stretch, while the top thread forms two parallel rows of stitches.

- Prepare the hem as you would for a topstitched hem.

- Select a 3.0mm/80 or 4.0mm/80 double needle appropriate to the fabric.

- Use two spools of thread on the top of the machine, positioning them so the threads unwind in opposite directions. This prevents the threads from tangling.

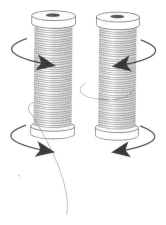

- Pass the threads through the machine tensions as if they were a single thread, separating them at the needles.

- For best results, lengthen the stitch and slightly loosen the tension. Test the stitching on a fabric scrap before stitching on the garment. Adjust the tension and stitch length if necessary.

NOTE *from* NANCY

If your machine does not have two spool pins, wind an extra bobbin and stack the bobbin with the spool on the spool pin.

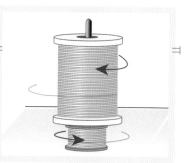

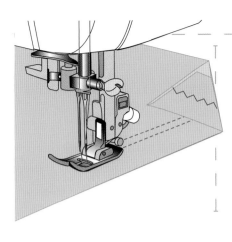

- Stitch a uniform distance from the hem fold, sewing on the right side of the fabric. Check to ensure the stitching catches the hem.

- Trim the excess hem fabric after completing the stitching.

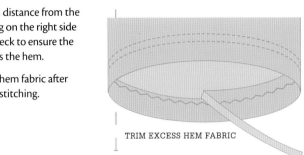

TRIM EXCESS HEM FABRIC

Easing: SEAMS

Whenever one of the seam edges is longer than the other (for example, on pants inseams, shoulder seams or curved princess-style seams), use the feed dogs to efficiently ease the fabric as you stitch the seam.

E

1 Place the longer seam edge next to the feed dogs, with the shorter edge on the top.

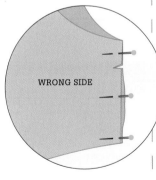

WRONG SIDE

2 Slightly cant the fabric up as you stitch to allow the feed dogs to bite more of the fabric and ease in the longer layer. Voilà! The edges of the finished seam match perfectly.

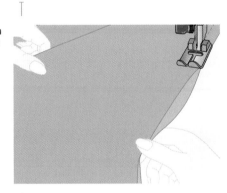

NOTE *from* NANCY

Ordinarily, we stitch directionally from the lower edge to the top edge of a garment seam. But if one seam edge is longer than the other, disregard that rule. Stitching directionally would mean that on one of the garment seams, the longer edge would be against the feed dogs, and on the other, the shorter edge would be against the feed dogs. Instead, in this case always sew with the longer length on the bottom, regardless of which direction you would be stitching.

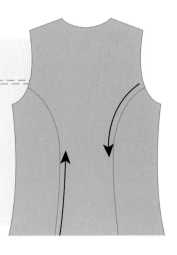

E

Use two pencils with erasers—and a little sewing know-how—to ease sleeves. Or choose one of the other methods for easing sleeves mentioned below.

Pencil Eraser Method

1 Place the cut-out sleeve under the presser foot, beginning at one of the underarm notches. Lower the needle into the fabric ½" (13mm) from the edge.

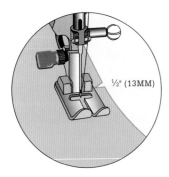

½" (13MM)

2 Position two pencil erasers on the fabric so one is on each side of the presser foot just in front of the needle. Pull the erasers outward and away from the presser foot as you stitch around the sleeve cap, stretching the fabric in front of the needle.

3 Sew over the eased area. Reposition the erasers and continue stitching, again pulling the erasers outward and away from the presser foot as you stitch around the sleeve cap.

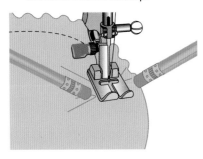

4 Repeat, stitching small sections at a time until you reach the underarm notch on the opposite edge of the sleeve.

Finger-Easing Method

This method requires only one row of stitching between notches and is perfect for lightweight to medium-weight fabrics. Practice on a fabric scrap until you get the hang of it.

1 Adjust the stitch length according to the fabric weight: 10–12 stitches per inch (per 2.5cm) for medium-weight fabrics and 12–14 stitches per inch (per 2.5cm) for lightweight.

2 Stitch ½" (13mm) from the cut edge of the sleeve cap.

3 Firmly press your finger against the back of the presser foot. Stitch 2" to 3" (5cm to 8cm), trying to stop the fabric from flowing through the machine. Release your finger and repeat.

- Your finger will prevent the flow of fabric from behind the presser foot, causing the feed dogs to ease each stitch slightly.

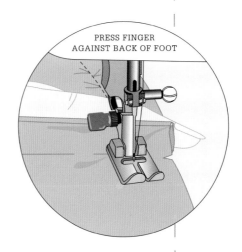

PRESS FINGER AGAINST BACK OF FOOT

Machine-Basting Method

A third option for easing is to machine-baste two rows of stitching between notches, stitching at ½" (13mm) and ¾" (19mm) from the edge. Ease the fabric by pulling the bobbin threads.

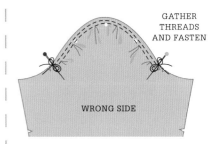

GATHER THREADS AND FASTEN

WRONG SIDE

To stitch picture-perfect pleats and tucks, or super-straight topstitching, use these edge-stitching techniques. An edgestitching foot is very helpful as it has an adjustable side bar designed with a lip to guide the fabric. It is the perfect guide for stitching even tucks.

E

NOTE from NANCY

If you use a marking pen or pencil, remember that pressing over those marks often makes them permanent or very difficult to remove. Mark only at the outer edges and then press to identify the entire length of the pleat or tuck.

1 Mark the outer edges of each pleat with a removable marking pen or pencil. Or cut short ¼" (6mm) nips at the outer edges to indicate pleat positions. Press-mark, wrong sides together, to identify each pleat position. Use the side or tip of the iron so you don't remove previously pressed pleat positions.

2 Determine the position for the side bar using test fabric.

- Mark the desired tuck distance from the fold.

- Position the fabric under the presser foot, lower the needle at the marked position and adjust the side bar so the folded fabric edge guides along the lip on the bar.

- To make tucks wider than ¼" (6mm), move the needle position to the left, if possible.

3 When the bar is positioned correctly, stitch the tucks on the project, beginning about ½" (13mm) from the cut edge to help the fabric feed through the machine. Guide the fabric over the lip and against the side bar.

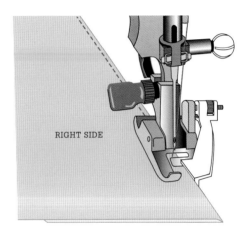

RIGHT SIDE

4 Repeat, stitching additional tucks at press-marked positions.

NOTE from NANCY

If you do not have an edgestitching foot, move the needle position to the far right side of a standard presser foot. Sew, guiding the foot along the edge of the fabric.

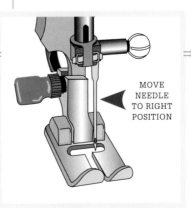

MOVE NEEDLE TO RIGHT POSITION

Tops, pants, dresses, swimwear, aerobic wear—the list is seemingly endless when it comes to using elastic as the hidden shaping secret. Here are the basic elastics that every creative person needs to know about.

Braided Elastic

- Strong, general-purpose elastic
- Sizes: ⅛"–⅜" (3mm–10mm)
- Fiber content: 100 percent polyester
- Use for fabric casings and swimwear

BRAIDED ELASTIC

Woven Elastic
(Non-Roll and Ribbed Non-Roll)

- Strong elastic that resists rolling and twisting
- Sizes: ½"–1" (13mm–25mm)
- Fiber content: 100 percent polyester
- Use for waistbands and other areas that require a strong elastic

RIBBED NON-ROLL ELASTIC

Knitted Elastic

- Soft and stretchy elastic
- Sizes: ½"–1½" (13mm–38mm)
- Fiber content: 67 percent polyester and 33 percent rubber
- Use mainly for knit sportswear and underwear

KNITTED ELASTIC

Heavy Stretch Waistband Elastic

- Heavy elastic that is soft and stretchy
- Size: 1½" (38mm)
- Fiber content: 65 percent polyester and 33 percent rubber
- Use primarily for waistbands in a casing (pages 31–32), or stitch it directly onto the fabric

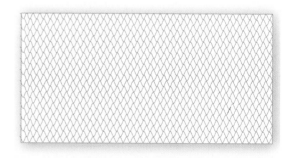

HEAVY STRETCH WAISTBAND ELASTIC

Clear Elastic

- Very stretchy: Stretches 3–4 times its original length
- Size: ⅜" (10mm)
- Fiber content: 100 percent polyurethane
- Use to stabilize knit seams or to finish neckline, armhole and leg openings on swimwear and activewear

CLEAR ELASTIC

There are a myriad of elastics and elastic techniques for use in garments and crafts. The following stitch-in elastic technique is a basic method with a variety of uses. If you prefer a traditional casing for elastic, see pages 31–32.

1 Prepare the elastic.

- Cut the elastic 2"–4" (5cm–10cm) smaller than the waistline measurement, depending on what you feel is comfortable.

- Anchor the elastic ends to woven fabric (page 32). Or, overlap the elastic ends ¼" (6mm). Zigzag the ends together several times. Use several rows of stitching to join the elastic securely.

NOTE *from* NANCY

If your waist is quite a bit smaller than your hips, pin the elastic together without trimming off the excess. Try on the elastic, pulling it up over your hips. If the elastic is too tight to slide comfortably over your hips, readjust the elastic before sewing it together.

2 Attach the elastic.

- Quarter both the elastic and the garment waistline; mark with pins or a fabric marker.

- Pin the elastic to the garment at each quarter point, meeting the elastic to the wrong side of the garment.

- Serge or zigzag the elastic to the cut edge of the waistband, stretching the elastic to fit.

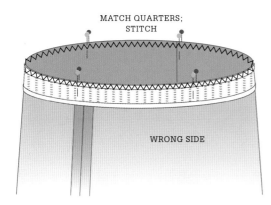

MATCH QUARTERS;
STITCH

WRONG SIDE

- Fold under the elastic for casing. Check to be sure the fabric is securely wrapped around the elastic.

- Baste stitch through the elastic and garment at each seam. This holds the casing and elastic in position for the final stitching. This stitching is removed after the casing is completed.

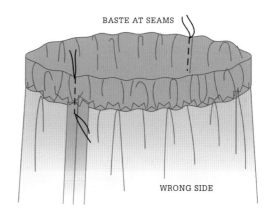

BASTE AT SEAMS

WRONG SIDE

- Straight stitch or zigzag along the lower edge of the casing, stretching the elastic to fit. Stitch around the entire waistline, using the initial zigzagging or serging as a guide. Remove the basting threads.

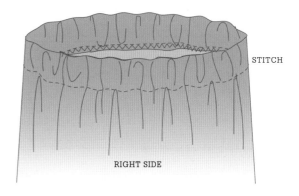

STITCH

RIGHT SIDE

E

Stabilize shoulder seams to prevent them from stretching out of shape. Use this clear elastic technique for a stretchy yet stable seam with good retention.

1 Cut a piece of clear elastic the length of the seam.

2 Stitch the clear elastic to the fabric using a narrow zigzag (.05–.1 width), often called a wobble stitch (page 60), or serge the seam, including the elastic in the seam.

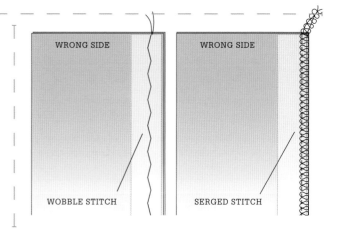

WRONG SIDE   WRONG SIDE

WOBBLE STITCH   SERGED STITCH

Fabric Tubes

F

The cylinders used to turn fabric tubes are ingenious and offer a simple time-saving solution to a job that once belonged to the lowly safety pin. After the hook connects with the fabric tube, one slick motion turns the tube right side out.

WRONG SIDE

1 Stitch the lengthwise edges of the tube together using a ¼" (6mm) seam, meeting right sides and leaving both ends unstitched. Finger press the seam open.

2 Select a fabric tube cylinder that slips easily inside the fabric tube.

• These cylindrical tubes are available in sizes ranging from ⅛"–¾" (3mm–19mm) openings. It's a two-part notion: a cylinder and a slender wire with a pigtail hook that inserts into the cylinder.

3 Turn the tube right-side-out.

• Slip the cylinder inside the stitched tube. Wrap and fold one end of the tube tightly over the end of the cylinder.

• Insert the wire into the cylinder from the handle end. Turn the hook clockwise (to the right) so the pigtail goes through the fabric.

INSERT WIRE AND TURN HOOK CLOCKWISE

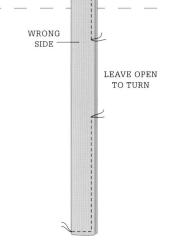

LEAVE OPEN TO TURN

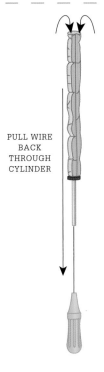

PULL WIRE BACK THROUGH CYLINDER

Add Cording or Stuffing to Tubes

1 Select cording that will fit inside the fabric tube, or cut strips of polyester fleece the width of the original fabric strip.

2 Cut, stitch and thread the tube over the cylinder. Insert the hook and pull the first ½" (13mm) of the fabric into the tube as detailed at left.

3 Tape the end of the cording to make insertion easier. With fleece, roll and tape the end to form a narrow point that will fit inside the tube.

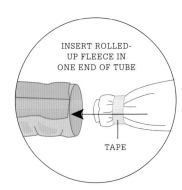

INSERT ROLLED-UP FLEECE IN ONE END OF TUBE

TAPE

Turn Longer Tubes

1 Turn large tubes with finished ends by stitching the ends of the tubes closed and leaving an opening in the middle of the tube.

2 Thread half of the fabric tube onto the appropriate fabric tube cylinder. Turn the tube right side out.

- Gently pull the wire back through the cylinder, turning the fabric tube right-side-out. Do not turn the hook or it may release from the fabric.

- When the turned tube reaches the opening in the cylinder, release the hook by turning it counterclockwise (to the left). Complete the turning by pulling the fabric, rather than the hook, to prevent the wire from breaking.

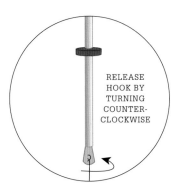

RELEASE HOOK BY TURNING COUNTER-CLOCKWISE

4 Insert the end of the cording/fleece into the end of the tube and gently pull on the hook. The cording/fleece will be drawn into the tube and automatically encased as the tube is turned.

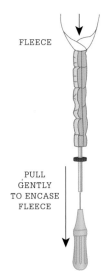

FLEECE

PULL GENTLY TO ENCASE FLEECE

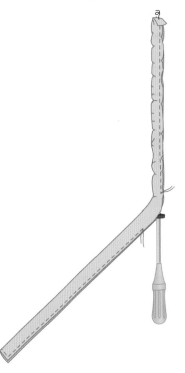

3 Repeat for the remaining half of the tube. Hand-stitch the opening closed.

F

A facing covers and encloses a raw edge. It usually doesn't show on the outside of the garment. You may find facings at the neckline, armhole, sleeve, and the front and back openings.

1 Fuse interfacing to the wrong side of the facing sections.

2 If the facing has several sections, follow the pattern directions for stitching them together. Press the seams open and trim them to ¼" (6mm) to reduce bulk.

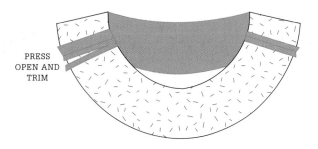

PRESS
OPEN AND
TRIM

3 Finish the outer edge of the facing by zigzagging, serging or clean finishing the edges.

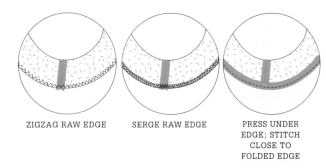

ZIGZAG RAW EDGE   SERGE RAW EDGE   PRESS UNDER
EDGE; STITCH
CLOSE TO
FOLDED EDGE

4 Stitch the facing to the garment, right sides together, aligning the cut edges and matching the notches, seams and markings.

NOTE *from* NANCY

Use pinking shears to grade and trim the seam allowances in one step. When using lightweight fabrics, trim both seam allowances simultaneously. To minimize bulk when using heavier fabrics, cut each seam allowance separately.

5 Cut each seam allowance a different width to reduce bulk all the way around the neckline. This is called grading.

• Trim the facing seam to ¼" (6mm).

• Trim the garment seam to ⅜" (10mm).

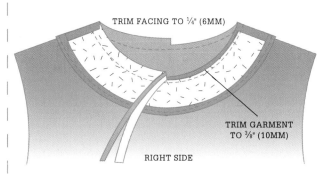

TRIM FACING TO ¼" (6MM)

TRIM GARMENT
TO ⅜" (10MM)

RIGHT SIDE

6 Understitch as follows, stitching both seam allowances to the facing. Understitching prevents the facing from rolling to the right side.

• Press the seam flat, then press the facing away from the garment, covering the seam allowance. Press all the seam allowances toward the facing.

• From the right side, stitch the seam allowances to the facing with either a straight stitch, zigzag or multi-step zigzag. Stitch on the facing close to the seamline.

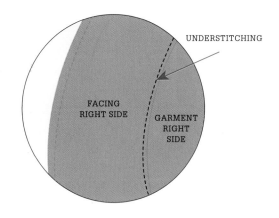

UNDERSTITCHING

FACING
RIGHT SIDE

GARMENT
RIGHT
SIDE

7 Turn the facing to the wrong side and press.

8 Secure the facing to the garment at the seamlines. Stitch in the ditch as follows to prevent the facing from rolling to the right side.

- Stitch in the groove (called the ditch) of each seam. Stitch from the right side, sewing through all the thicknesses.

- Pull the thread tails to the wrong side and tie. Clip off the thread tails.

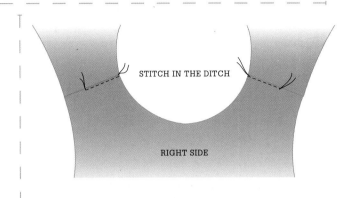

STITCH IN THE DITCH

RIGHT SIDE

Fusible Web

Fusible web is available by the yard or on a narrow roll. Sandwich fusible web between two layers of fabric and press to secure, following the manufacturer's instructions. Fusible web usually forms a permanent bond, securing the fabric layers together. Fusible web is often used for emergency hemming.

F

Fusible Web: PAPER-BACKED

Paper-backed fusible web has one side that is a fusible web and the other is a paper backing. Pressing on the paper side of the fusible web adheres the web to fabric, securely positioning it for stitching. Fusible webs are available in various weights. Test to find one that works best for the fabric and the project.

F

G

Gathers add an attractive accent to a project, but preventing gathering threads from breaking and getting the gathers evenly distributed can be challenging. Although there are several ways to gather fabric, once you try my favorite technique, there's no need to try any other method.

1 Place the fabric to be gathered under the presser foot, positioning the needle ½"–⅝" (13mm–16mm) from the edge. Turn the wheel by hand or press the one stitch button to take one complete stitch in the fabric.

2 Lightly pull on the top thread and draw up the loop that appears. Bring the bobbin thread to the top of the fabric.

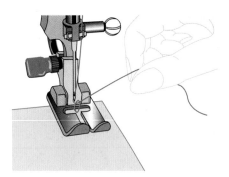

3 Grasp both the top and bobbin threads. Pull the threads to measure as long as the area to be gathered. Gently twist the two threads together and position them under the presser foot.

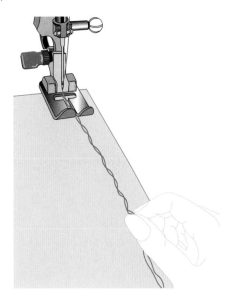

4 Adjust the sewing machine for a medium zigzag with the stitch length and width set at approximately 3. Zigzag over the twisted threads inside the seam allowance, making a casing for the gathering threads. Be sure you don't stitch through the twisted threads! Stop stitching ⅝" (16mm) from the edge.

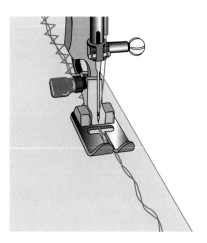

5 Gather the fabric by gently pulling on the twisted threads. Because the threads are anchored in the first stitch, they will not pull out of the fabric. Wrap the thread tails around a pin after the fabric is gathered to the appropriate size.

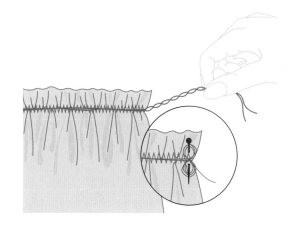

The technique of grading a seam can be found in the earliest of sewing textbooks. The process is simple—a sewing mainstay!

G

Grade seam allowances by trimming each seam allowance to a different width. Grade seams such as collars, cuffs and neckline seams to reduce the bulk and help the seams lie flat. Usually the garment seam allowance is left the widest. For example, when trimming a facing, trim the facing allowance to ¼" (6mm) and the garment seam allowance to ⅜" (10mm).

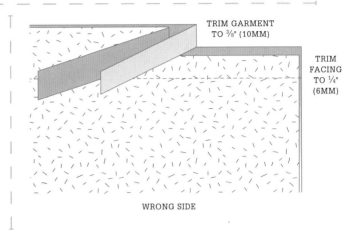

TRIM GARMENT TO ⅜" (10MM)

TRIM FACING TO ¼" (6MM)

WRONG SIDE

Grainline

The grainline on the pattern—the longest linear line printed on the piece—is given to align with the grainline of the fabric. Matching the grainlines of the pattern and the fabric will ensure that the garment will fit and hang properly.

G

A straight line with an arrow on each end is the symbol used for grainline. Use this arrow to position the pattern on the fabric. The grainline arrow should run parallel to the selvage edge of the fabric, or the lengthwise grain of the fabric. For more detailed information, see pages 64–65.

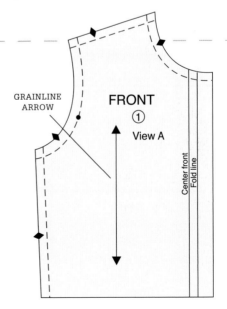

GRAINLINE ARROW

FRONT
①
View A

Center front
Fold line

H

Make half-square triangles by taking two fabric squares, sewing diagonally with right sides together, then cutting the squares in half diagonally between the stitching lines. Voilà—two half-square triangles!

1 Select two contrasting fabrics and cut block sizes from each as follows: (Includes ¼" [6mm] seam allowances on all edges.)

- For a 3½" (9cm) block: Cut 3⅞" (10cm) squares.

- For a 4½" (11cm) block: Cut 4⅞" (12cm) squares.

- For a 6½" (17cm) block: Cut 6⅞" (18cm) squares.

2 Place the two contrasting squares right sides together.

3 Mark a diagonal line from one corner to the opposite corner, and mark ¼" (6mm) seam allowances on each side of the diagonal line.

WRONG SIDE

4 Stitch on each of the marked seam allowance lines.

5 Cut the squares apart on the diagonal line between the seam allowances.

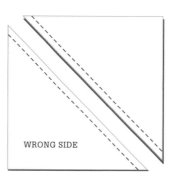

WRONG SIDE

6 Press both sections open to create two half-square triangles.

NOTE *from* NANCY

I like to use a Quick Quarter for ease in marking half-square triangles. The center slot provides an accurate opening for marking the diagonal line, and the edges provide perfect ¼" (6mm) seam allowances on both sides.

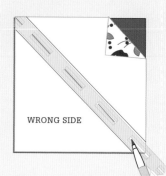

WRONG SIDE

Nearly everything you sew has a hem—skirts, pants, sleeves and even home décor items such as curtains and table linens. By using a few simple hints, you can turn this time-consuming chore into a simple sewing task.

1 Fold up the hem.

- Prepress the hem on each flat piece before stitching it to another piece. This is a great time-saving technique.

- Use a hem gauge, such as the Ezy-Hem Gauge to provide an accurate measurement and to avoid leaving a hem impression on the right side of the fabric. Place the gauge on the wrong side of the fabric. Fold up the hem allowances over the gauge to the desired width and press.

2 Grade the seam allowances within the hem area to reduce bulk.

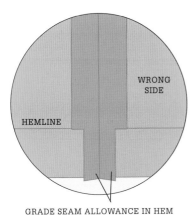

GRADE SEAM ALLOWANCE IN HEM

3 Finish the cut edge of the hem by zigzagging or serging.

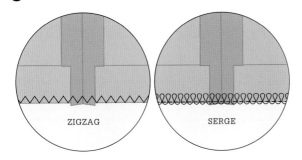

ZIGZAG   SERGE

4 Hand-stitch the hem in place using a blind hem stitch.

- Thread a needle with a single strand of thread. Cut the thread about 18" (46cm) long. The thread will tangle and knot more easily if it is too long. Knot one end of the thread.

- Fold back the hem edge so ¼" (6mm) of the edge shows.

- Work from right to left.

- Take a tiny stitch in the hem; then take a tiny stitch in the project about ¼" (6mm) ahead of that stitch. Pick up only one or two threads in the fabric.

- Take a stitch in the hem edge about ¼" (6mm) ahead of the last stitch.

- Repeat, alternating stitches between the hem edge and the project. Don't pull the stitches too tight or the hem will pucker.

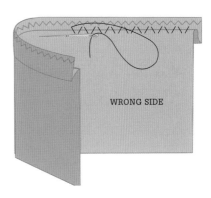

continued on next page >

5 As an option, stitch the hem using a machine blind hem stitch.

- Fold back the project edge so about ¼" (6mm) of the hem edge shows.

- Adjust your sewing machine for a blind hem stitch as detailed in your owner's manual.

- Stitch so the straight stitch falls in the hem allowance and the zig just catches the project at the fold.

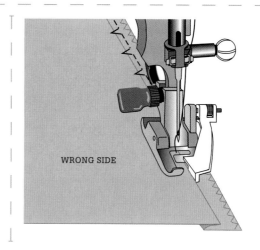

WRONG SIDE

Hooks and Eyes

H

Use hooks and eyes to fasten garment openings where there will be lots of stress, such as on waistbands. Use a straight eye when the edges overlap and a looped eye when the edges only meet. Regular hooks and eyes are available in sizes 0–3, with 3 being the largest.

1 Sew on the hook.

- Place the hook on the overlap with its end (the bill) about ⅛" (3mm) from the edge.

- Use a single, knotted thread. Fasten the thread under the hook.

- Stitch around both rings, placing the stitches close together. Stitch through only the facing and interfacing. Do not stitch through to the right side of the garment.

- Before fastening the thread, fasten the bill with several over-hand stitches. This helps keep the top layer flat when the hook is fastened.

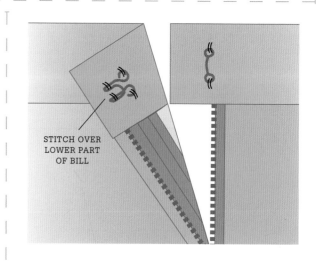

STITCH OVER
LOWER PART
OF BILL

2 Sew on the eye.

- Position the hook over the other part of the garment as if it were fastened.

- Place the straight eye or the loop of the rounded eye directly under the hook. Mark its position.

- Stitch around the rings of the eye.

Interfacings are hidden inside garments, but they're essential for good construction. Fused or sewn to the wrong side of the fabric, interfacing adds shape and body.

Choosing the Right Weight and Type of Interfacing for Your Fabric

- **Nonfusible interfacing** is generally basted in place and is later secured in place as the pieces are stitched together.

- **Fusible interfacing** is easier to work with and therefore is better suited to beginning sewers.

  - Choose a fusible interfacing that is one weight lighter than your fabric since the fusing resins add weight once the interfacing is fused to the fabric.

  - There are three general categories of fusible interfacing: nonwoven, woven and knit.

  - Each category of fusible interfacing is available in light-weight to midweight.

Storing Interfacing

- To store interfacing, roll it onto a tube. This prevents wrinkles and saves space. Tuck the interfacing instructions for fusing inside the tube.

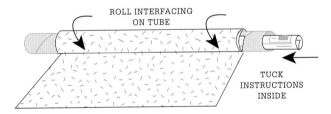

ROLL INTERFACING ON TUBE

TUCK INSTRUCTIONS INSIDE

NOTE *from* NANCY

Before purchasing interfacing, feel the weight and think, "Less is best!" A weight lighter than the fabric often provides the perfect shaping. When in doubt, press a sample of fusible interfacing on a sample of fabric. You'll know in seconds if you've chosen the correct weight.

There are times when a fusible interfacing isn't the best choice—when working with silk fabric in particular! In that instance, I often cut a second layer of the silk to use as the interfacing. Machine- or hand-baste the second layer of silk in place for a drapable, yet supportive interfacing.

Using Fusible Interfacing for a Fuss-Free Interfacing Application

- Interface the entire fabric piece. This is called a full fuse. Cut interfacing to the pattern size.

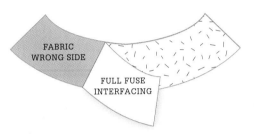

FABRIC WRONG SIDE

FULL FUSE INTERFACING

- Center the interfacing on the fabric, placing the rough side of the interfacing (the side with the glue dots) next to the wrong side of the fabric.

- Cover the interfacing with a damp press cloth.

- Use the tip of your iron to steam-baste the interfacing, securing it to the fabric in a few key areas.

- Fuse the interfacing following the manufacturer's instructions.

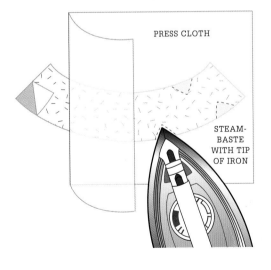

PRESS CLOTH

STEAM-BASTE WITH TIP OF IRON

J

Give an unlined jacket all the benefits of a lining without all the work with this quick pattern change. Extending the facing adds support and shaping, hides shoulder pads and keeps facings in place.

1 Modify the front facing pattern.

- Pin the front facing pattern to the front jacket pattern, matching the notches.

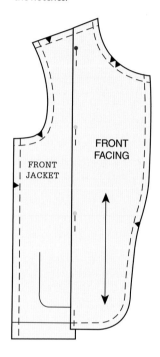

FRONT JACKET

FRONT FACING

- Place a length of waxed paper, tissue paper or pattern tracing paper over the pattern pieces.

- Use a pen to extend the shoulder cutting line of the facing to the armhole. Next, measure down and trace 2"–3" (5cm–8cm) along the armhole cutting line. From that point, gradually taper the cutting line back to the original facing line, providing a smooth curve.

- Tape the pattern extension to the facing pattern.

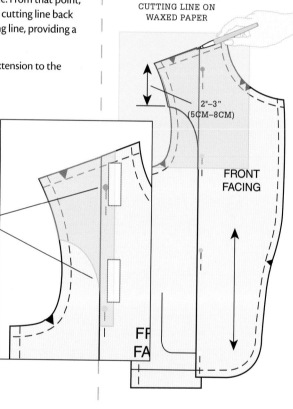

EXTEND SHOULDER LINE AND ARMHOLE CUTTING LINE ON WAXED PAPER

2"–3" (5CM–8CM)

FRONT FACING

TAPE EXTENSION IN PLACE

FR FA

2 Prepare a back facing pattern.

- Pin the back facing pattern to the back jacket pattern.

- Place waxed paper, tissue paper or pattern tracing paper over the pattern pieces. (If the pattern does not have a back facing, place the paper directly over the jacket pattern.)

- Trace the shoulder seams from neckline to armhole.

- Measure down and trace 2"–3" (5cm–8cm) on the armhole cutting line. From that point, mark straight across to the center back.

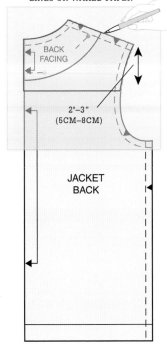

TRACE NEW FACING
LINES ON WAXED PAPER

BACK
FACING

2"–3"
(5CM–8CM)

JACKET
BACK

- Cut the pattern, placing the center back on the fold.

3 Prepare the facings.

- Cut fabric and interfacing from the modified front and back facing patterns. Fuse interfacing to the wrong side of the fabric following the manufacturer's instructions.

- Stitch the facing shoulder seams and press the seams open.

STITCH FACING
SHOULDER SEAMS

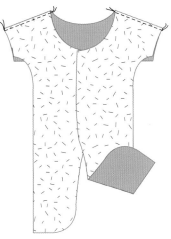

- Serge the facing edges to finish them and prevent raveling.

- Join the facings to the jacket following the pattern instructions.

- Turn the facings to the inside of the jacket and secure them in place by tacking them to the armhole seam allowances.

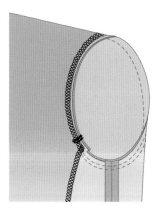

J

Here's a fast lining technique that gives jacket sleeves additional body and makes the jacket easier to slip on over a blouse or sweater. You can fully line and hem the sleeve in one step, even if the pattern doesn't call for a lining.

1 Verify the sleeve length.

- Because the sleeve is lined and hemmed simultaneously, it is important that the pattern is altered to the correct length prior to cutting.

- Double-check arm length against the pattern's sleeve length. Lengthen or shorten the pattern as needed.

2 Create the lined sleeve.

- Cut out the fashion fabric sleeves (including any alterations made). Interface the hem area if desired.

WRONG SIDE

- Fold under the hem allowance on the sleeve pattern to make the lining pattern. Cut out the lining using this modified pattern.

FASHION FABRIC   LINING

- With right sides together, join the sleeve and lining at the hem edge using a ⅝" (16mm) seam.

- Grade the seam, trimming the lining seam allowance to ¼" (6mm) and the jacket allowance to ⅜" (10mm).

- Press the seam flat, then toward the lining.

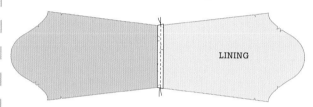

LINING

- Prepress the sleeve hemline using a hem gauge, such as an Ezy-Hem Gauge. (This is easy to do while the sleeve is still flat, and it saves time later.) Place the gauge on the wrong side of the fabric. Fold up the hem allowance over the gauge to the desired hemline and press. By using the gauge, you also avoid leaving an imprint on the right side of the fabric.

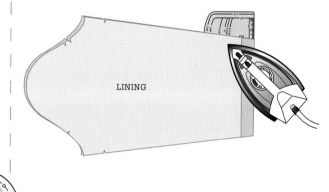

LINING

- Place the underarm seams of the lining and the sleeve right sides together, matching the seam intersection.

- Stitch the entire underarm seam. Press the seam flat and then open using a sleeve roll to prevent an imprint.

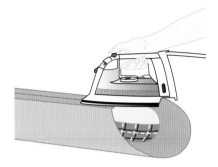

- Reach inside the sleeve; grasp the fashion fabric and the lining at the hemline. Turn the sleeve right side out, aligning the armhole edges.

- Zigzag or serge the sleeve caps together. Handle the two layers as one when inserting the sleeve into the garment.

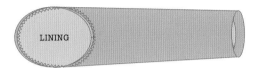

LINING

Knit: IDENTIFICATION

Sewing knit fashions can be a very speedy process and one that's truly creative and enjoyable. Selecting an appropriate knit fabric for the pattern you're using is essential because different types of knits have different amounts of stretch.

K

To determine if a fabric is appropriate, test the crosswise stretch of the fabric from selvage to selvage using the knit guide on the pattern.

- Position a section of the fabric over the knit guide. Securely hold the knit at the left edge of the guide.

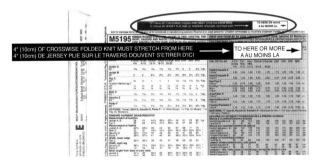

- With your right hand, grasp the fabric at the distance indicated on the fabric (generally about 4" [10cm]).

- Stretch the knit. It must stretch to the second position on the guide to be suitable.

KNIT MUST STRETCH TO SECOND GUIDE POSITION

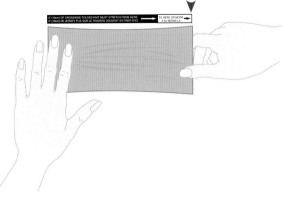

The beauty of sewing knits is that there are very few rules to follow. The sewing is truly simple!

Seaming Knit Fabric with a Sewing Machine

- Use a ballpoint or a stretch needle. The specially designed tip pushes the loops of the knit fabric apart, rather than stitching through them.

- Thread the machine top and bobbin with polyester thread.

- For stable knits, use two rows of stitching: a straight stitch followed by a zigzag. If the pattern includes a ⅝" (16mm) seam allowance, trim the seam allowance to ¼" (6mm).

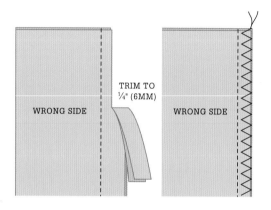

TRIM TO ¼" (6MM)

WRONG SIDE   WRONG SIDE

- For knits with greater stretch, use a *wobble stitch*. This stitch is really important when stitching slinky knits with a conventional sewing machine, but it can also be used on other knits with moderate stretch.

  – Adjust the machine for a zigzag with the stitch width set at 0.5mm and stitch length at 3.5mm.

  – Stitch the seam.

  – *Optional*: Zigzag edges together with a wider zigzag.

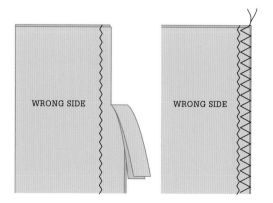

WRONG SIDE   WRONG SIDE

Seaming Knit Fabric with a Serger

- Use a 4-thread overlock (page 108).

- Position the pins parallel to the seam allowance to avoid hitting the blade mechanism.

WRONG SIDE

- For patterns with a ⅝" (16mm) seam allowance, align the edge of the fabric along the marking appropriate on your serger. For patterns with ¼" (6mm) seam allowances, align the edge of the fabric with the blade.

- Serge, trimming any seam allowance in excess of ¼" (6mm).

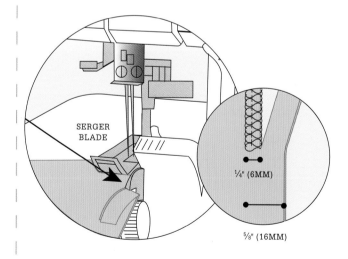

SERGER BLADE

¼" (6MM)

⅝" (16MM)

The following are some common knit fabrics and their characteristics. Be sure to choose a knit suited for the pattern you have selected.

K

Single Knit

- Lightweight; ideal for tops
- One side resembles a knit stitch; the other looks like interlocking loops

Interlock

- Lightweight, but heavier than single knits (A lighter version of a double knit, often 50 percent polyester/50 percent cotton)
- Lots of stretch in the crosswise grain, but little or none in the lengthwise grain

Double Knit

- Heavier and beefier than interlock
- Looks the same on both front and back
- Stretches crosswise, but is stable lengthwise

Knits Containing Spandex

- Very roomy fabric
- Significant stretch in the crosswise grain and some stretch in the lengthwise grain

Raschel Knit

- A lightweight textured knit

Slinky Knit

- Lightweight and very stretchy (Almost 100 percent stretch in width and about 50 percent stretch in length)
- Often a blend of 90 percent acetate or nylon and 10 percent spandex
- Doesn't wrinkle; great for travel

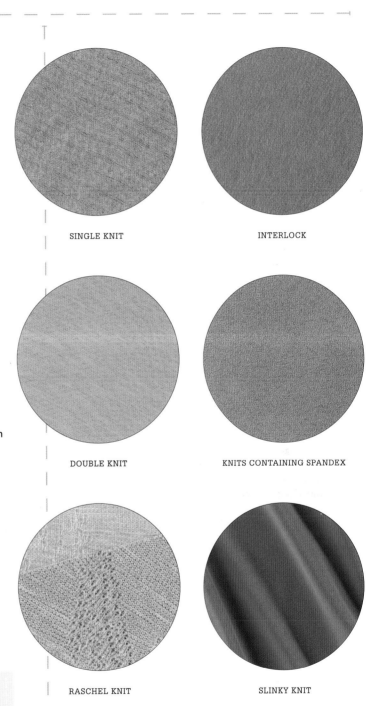

SINGLE KNIT

INTERLOCK

DOUBLE KNIT

KNITS CONTAINING SPANDEX

RASCHEL KNIT

SLINKY KNIT

NOTE *from* NANCY

If the knit fabric is all or part cotton, prewash the fabric before cutting out the garment to remove any residual shrinkage as well as any sizing that may have been applied during manufacturing.

L

In making most quilts, the layers of backing, batting and quilt top are pinned together to secure them for quilting. Here are several options to choose from.

1 Cut the backing fabric and batting approximately 3" (8cm) larger than the quilt top on all sides.

2 Place the backing wrong-side-up on a firm clean surface.

3 Securely tape the backing to the surface, using Sewer's Fix-It Tape or masking tape.

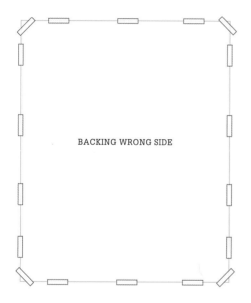

BACKING WRONG SIDE

4 Choose the batting that is best suited for your quilt.

5 Center the batting over the backing and smooth the surface so that it lies flat.

6 Center the quilt top right-side-up over the batting.

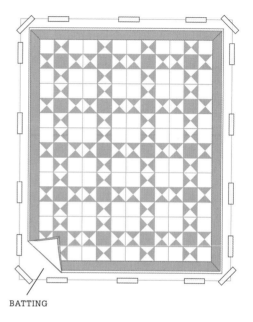

BATTING

7 Choose one of the following options for securing the layers:

• Spray baste the quilt layers.

– Select an acid-free temporary adhesive basting spray.

– Follow the directions on the packaging to layer the top, batting and backing without pins or hand basting. Adhesive basting spray holds fabric firmly, yet the fabric can be easily repositioned.

- Pin the quilt layers.

  - Using size 1 curved basting pins, start pinning at the center and work toward the outer edges.

  - Place pins 3"–4" (8cm–10cm) apart and no closer than ½" (13mm) from the seams to allow room for the presser foot when machine quilting.

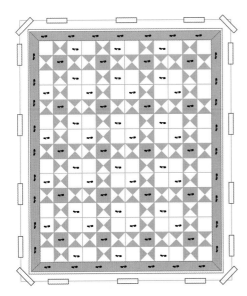

NOTE *from* NANCY

Use the Kwik Klip in combination with your safety pins when pinning. It helps close the pins to cut down on basting time; plus it helps avoid sore fingers and hand fatigue.

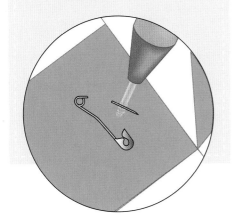

- Fuse baste the quilt layers.

  - Fuse ½" (13mm) squares of paper-backed fusible web (with the paper still attached) to the backing, positioning them every 4"–5" (10cm–13cm) (about a fist width) apart.

  - Remove the paper backing and position the batting over the quilt backing.

  - Fuse ½" (13mm) squares of paper-backed fusible web to the wrong side of the quilt top as detailed above.

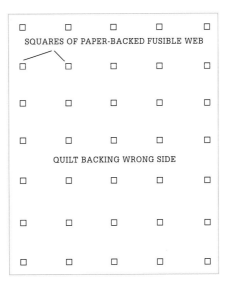

SQUARES OF PAPER-BACKED FUSIBLE WEB

QUILT BACKING WRONG SIDE

  - Position the quilt top over the batting.

  - Press to fuse all the layers together. The fusible web will secure the layers, so it won't be necessary to pin through the fabric layers.

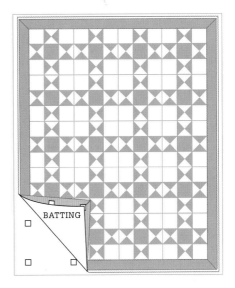

BATTING

L

Accurately laying out the pattern is an essential part of constructing any project. The pattern guide sheet provides lots of valuable information. Here are a few additional time-saving tips.

1 Roughly position all pattern pieces on the fabric. The illustration features a one-way layout, ideal for napped fabrics and knits.

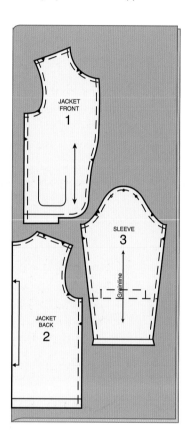

- Position all pieces that need to be placed on the fold.

- Secure the grainline of the other pattern pieces using only two pins.

  – Pin one end of the grainline arrow; measure from the arrow to the fold.

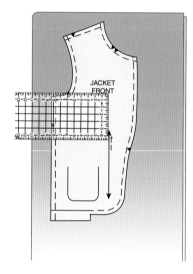

  – Shift the pattern as necessary until the other end of the arrow measures the same distance. Pin that end of the grainline to the fabric.

- Pin the grainlines of all pattern pieces. Do not pin the outer edges of the pattern.

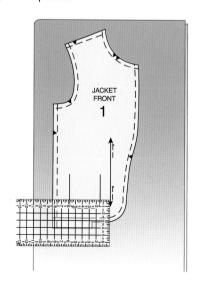

NOTE *from* NANCY

For greatest accuracy, I like to extend the pattern grainline so it's visible the entire length of the pattern. Fold the tissue pattern along the grainline arrow and press with a dry iron to extend the line the full length of the pattern. I also find that using an acrylic ruler to measure the grainline is faster and more accurate than using a tape measure.

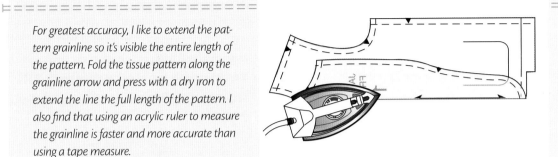

2 If the fabric does not have a one-way direction or nap, place straight cutting lines adjacent to each other when possible.

• This *sharing* technique saves cutting time, since you're actually cutting two edges at once.

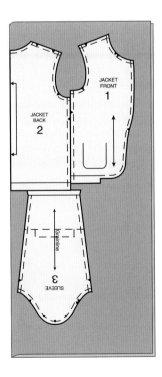

3 Use weights to secure the remaining pattern edges.

• Position the weights near the edges of one piece and cut it out. Then, reposition the weights on another pattern piece and cut.

• Repeat until all pieces are cut.

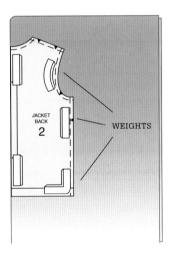

NOTE *from* NANCY

Consider substituting small cans, such as tuna cans, for pattern weights.

Use a roll of transparent or translucent tape to create perfect mitered corners on patch pockets. Does it sound impossible? Here's how!

1 Measure and mark twice the seam width from each side of the corner.

- For example, with ⅝" (16mm) seams, mark 1¼" (3cm) on each side of the corner.

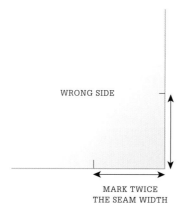

WRONG SIDE

MARK TWICE
THE SEAM WIDTH

2 Place a strip of tape, such as Sewer's Fix-It Tape, on the wrong side of the fabric between the two marks, extending the tape at each edge.

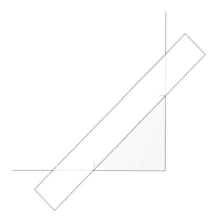

3 Fold the corner to a point, right sides together, aligning the marks and the tape.

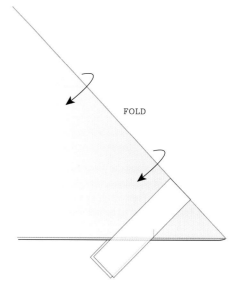

FOLD

4 Stitch from mark to mark, following the tape edge.

5 Remove the tape. Trim the seam to ¼" (6mm).

6 Turn the corner right-side-out. Press. Repeat as needed to miter all corners.

WRONG SIDE

Mitered borders are commonly used on art quilts. Like a picture frame showcases a photo, the mitered borders frame a quilt.

1 Cut the borders.

- Cut borders ½" (13mm) wider than the desired finished width of the border.

- Cut two borders a minimum of 8" (20cm) longer than the side measurement of the quilt.

- Cut another two borders at least 8" (20cm) longer than the top and bottom measurement of the quilt.

2 Pin the borders to the sides of the quilt top, right sides together, allowing equal amounts of excess strip length at each end of the quilt.

3 Stitch the borders to the quilt.

- Place a mark on the side borders ¼" (6mm) from each corner of the quilt.

- Stitch from mark to mark using a ¼" (6mm) seam.

BORDER WRONG SIDE

PRESS BORDERS OUT

4 Repeat, pinning and stitching the borders to the top and bottom of the quilt, again stopping ¼" (6mm) from each corner and allowing 3"–4" (8cm–10cm) extensions at each end.

5 Form the miters, working with one corner at a time.

- Press the borders right side out to their finished position.

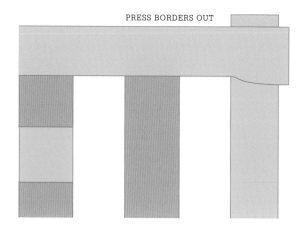

PRESS BORDERS OUT

- Smooth one of the corner borders flat.

- Fold the adjoining border, aligning the outer edges of the two border strips to create a 45-degree mitered corner. Press along the fold.

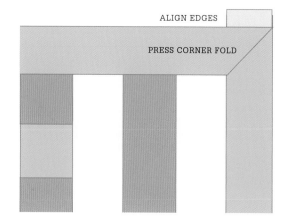

ALIGN EDGES

PRESS CORNER FOLD

- Pin the borders together at the mitered edge. Fold back the quilt top, exposing the wrong side and the press mark.

- Stitch along the press mark, sewing to the point of the miter. Trim seam allowances to ¼" (6mm).

- Press the seam open.

- Repeat, mitering each corner.

Nap

Fabrics that have a nap include mohair, brushed denim, fleece, chenille, corduroy, terry, velvet and velveteen. Because of the way they're woven, these fabrics reflect light differently from different positions. Here are the guidelines to use when working with napped fabrics. Cut all pattern pieces with the tops facing in the same direction. You usually need more fabric to accommodate this special layout. Patterns that suggest napped fabrics usually provide napped layout diagrams and indicate extra yardage requirements.

N

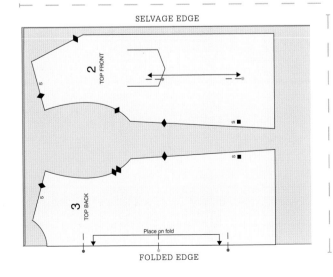

Special Instructions for Napped Fabrics

- Take special care when pressing napped fabrics. Use a press cloth, and press from the wrong side. Test the heat, the amount of steam and the pressure on scraps before pressing your project.

- Stitch in the direction of the nap.

N

Use a needle that is designed to work with the type and weight of fabric you are stitching and with the kind of project you are sewing.

Anatomy of a Needle

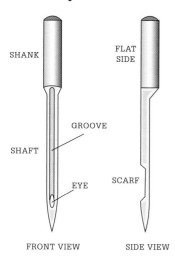

FRONT VIEW   SIDE VIEW

NOTE *from* NANCY

To reduce the possibility of bending or breaking the needle, stop stitching with the needle out of the fabric and raise the presser foot. Remove the fabric by gently moving it to the side and back of the sewing machine, and then cutting the threads.

- **Shank**—the larger diameter top of the needle that is inserted into the needle bar. The back of the shank is flat to aid in correctly inserting the needle.

- **Shaft**—the smaller diameter, lower part of the needle that goes through the fabric during stitching.

- **Groove**—an indentation on the shaft of the needle in which the thread rests.

- **Scarf**—the indentation on the back of the needle, just above the eye, that holds the thread during stitch formation.

- **Eye**—the hole through which the needle is threaded.

- **Point**—the tip of the needle. Different points (universal, ballpoint, jeans, etc.) are suited for particular fabrics and threads.

Scarves

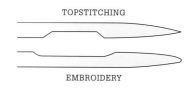

TOPSTITCHING

EMBROIDERY

Points and Eyes

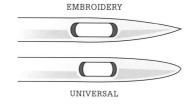

EMBROIDERY

UNIVERSAL

Understanding Different Needles

- Use a ballpoint needle with knit fabrics and a sharp needle with wovens. If you are using a specialty thread, select a needle to work with that thread. Use a denim needle for jeans, a Metafil needle for metallic thread and an embroidery needle for rayon embroidery thread.

- Needles are sized using either American and/or European systems.

  - **European sizes:**
    60   70   80   90   100   110

  - **American sizes:**
    8   10   12   14   16   18

- Sometimes a needle package lists both sizes, such as 80/12. Remember that the smaller the number, the finer the needle. The finer the fabric and the thread, the smaller the needle size should be. A smaller needle will place less stress on the fabric.

- Insert a new needle at the start of each sewing project, or after eight hours of sewing. The flat side of the needle rests against the needle bar. Also, be sure to change the needle whenever it is bent, dull or develops a burr.

Mark notches, outer edges of darts, center fronts and center backs, pleats and hemlines with short nips.

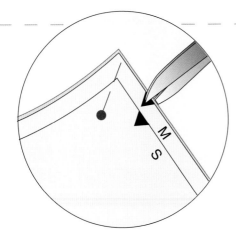

A nip is a ⅛"–¼" (3mm–6mm) long clip into the seam allowance, perpendicular to the seamline. The important part is the length of the clip—don't cut too far! If you do, you will weaken the seam or have a hole in your project.

Notches

Notches are shown on a pattern as single, double or triple diamonds. They help match fabric pieces accurately as you sew.

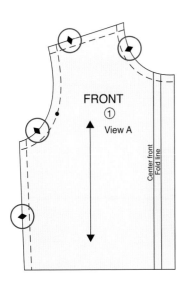

FRONT
①
View A

Center front
Fold line

1 Cut notches even with the cutting line of the pattern.

- Cut even with the cutting line to produce a smoother line.
- Notches can be marked or nipped at a later point.

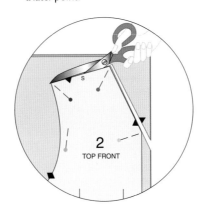

2
TOP FRONT

2 Mark the notches.

- An easy way to mark notches is with a washable marking pen or chalk pencil.
- Mark the notch with a short line perpendicular to the cut edge.
- If you prefer to nip, see above.

2
TOP FRONT

O

Keeping fabric organized had always been a challenge for me until my friends in the Nancy's Notions fabric warehouse suggested that similar sizes of fabric can be stored and stacked with ease. Here's a quick way to organize lengths and partial cuts of fabric.

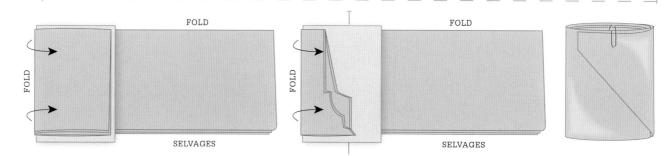

FOLD · FOLD · SELVAGES · FOLD · FOLD · SELVAGES

1 Fold a length of fabric in half lengthwise, aligning the fabric's fold to the selvages.

2 Place a pocket folder or piece of cardboard measuring approximately 9" × 12" (23cm × 30cm) on top of the fabric. Wrap the length of fabric around the form. If your fabric has been partially used, wrap that end around the form first.

3 Once you reach the end of the fabric, tuck the end under diagonally and secure it with a bobby pin or clip. Remove the folder/cardboard.

O

Use this sewing notion standby, the tomato pincushion, to organize slightly used sewing machine needles. Marking the pincushion takes just minutes, yet the technique makes it so easy to organize and store needles.

Organize by Needle Size

- Use a felt-tipped marker to label various sections of the pincushion for specific needle sizes.

- When you remove a needle that's still usable from the sewing machine, place it in the appropriate section of the pincushion. When you again want to use a needle of a specific size, you can easily locate it in the pincushion.

Organize by Needle Type

- Also consider segmenting pincushions for various types of specialty needles. For example, there might be sections for different sizes of embroidery needles, denim needles, quilting needles, topstitching needles, etc.

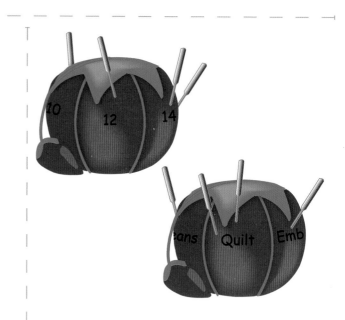

Finding a particular piece of a pattern will be a lot easier when you use this simple organizing technique.

1 After you're finished using pattern pieces, fold the pieces to a size that will fit in the pattern envelope, making certain that the pattern number and the name of the pattern piece are visible on the outside.

2 Press with a dry iron.

3 For especially convenient viewing, store the pattern pieces in a transparent plastic bag. The outer portion conveniently holds the pattern envelope so you can easily reference yardages or other pertinent pattern information.

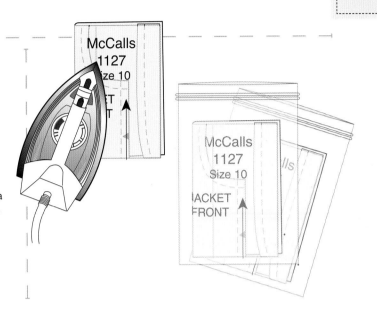

Organizing: PROJECTS

This organizational technique is perfect for keeping quilting or sewing projects under control. It organizes and tidies up your creative area in mere minutes.

1 Use a piece of fleece or batting large enough to easily hold the collection of quilt components. Place the fleece/batting on a flat surface such as a cutting table.

2 Position the quilting components on the fleece/batting. The quilting fabrics adhere to the textured surface of the fleece/batting.

3 Roll up the batting for easy storage or transport when you're finished quilting for the day.

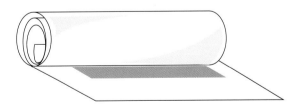

4 Unroll the batting when you want to resume work on the project. Everything will be secured as it was originally positioned.

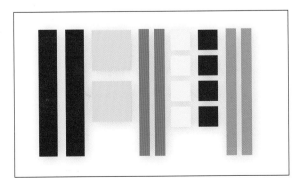

P

During my first year on television, I demonstrated this technique for making an easy lined patch pocket. It's stood the test of time: The pocket is accurately shaped, and the lining supports the pocket and prevents bagging and sagging.

1 Add a lining to the pocket.

- Fold under the top hem allowance of the pattern.
- Use that revised pattern as the pattern for the pocket lining.

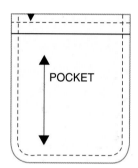
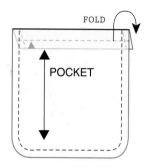

- Cut out the lining on the bias to avoid raveling.

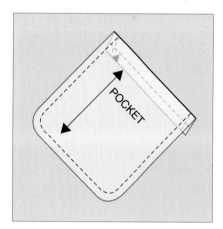

- Join hem edges of the lining and the pocket with a ⅝" (16mm) seam, right sides together. Press the seam open.

LINING WRONG SIDE

2 Prepress the outer pocket to the finished size.

- Press under the ⅝" (16mm) hem allowance using a hem gauge, such as the Ezy-Hem Gauge. Place short ¼" (6mm) nips at the hem foldline to mark its position.
- Press under the ⅝" (16mm) seam allowances on the pocket's outer curved edges. Then press under seam allowances on the remaining pocket edges.

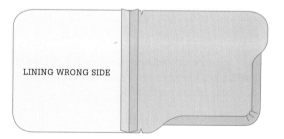

LINING WRONG SIDE

NOTE *from* NANCY

If the pocket fabric is bulky, trim the pocket seam allowances in corner areas to more easily shape the pocket, reduce bulk and eliminate seam allowance show-through.

3 Position and stitch the pocket to the garment.

- Position the pocket on the garment, aligning the hem nips with the pocket's marked upper edge.

- Flip up the fashion fabric pocket. Pin the lining to the garment.

- Mark a 1" (25mm) seam allowance on the lining. **This is important!**

- Adjust the machine for a zigzag stitch, using a narrow stitch width and a short stitch length.

- Stitch the lining to the garment, beginning at ⅝" (16mm) at the hem and tapering to the marked 1" (25mm) line. Taper back to ⅝" (16mm) at the second side of the pocket top.

POCKET
WRONG SIDE

- Trim away the excess seam allowance from the lining, trimming close to the zigzag stitching using an appliqué scissors. The pelican-shaped bill of this scissors makes it easier to trim the excess fabric close to the stitching line without nicking the fabric. Position the rounded blade under the fabric and trim.

- Turn down the fashion fabric pocket to cover the lining.

- Topstitch the fashion fabric pocket in place, reinforcing the stitching at upper corners of the pocket.

TOPSTITCH

P

Pintucks are delicate rows of double stitching often added to heirloom projects. Take the guesswork out of creating even rows of these tucks by combining a pintuck foot with a double needle.

1 Spray-starch the fabric for ease in sewing.

2 Set up the sewing machine.

- Attach a pintuck foot. This foot is grooved on the underside with five or more channels, offering the ability to sew everything from heirloom-sized details to larger-sized embellishments.

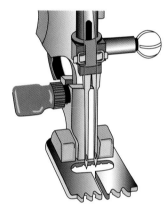

PINTUCK FOOT

- Insert a double needle. A double needle can be used on any zigzag machine that threads from front to back.

DOUBLE NEEDLE

- The first number of a double-needle size designation refers to the distance in millimeters between the two needles, while the second refers to the size of the needle itself. The smaller the number, the finer the needle.

- Use a 1.6mm/80, a 2.0mm/80 or a 2.5mm/80 needle with a 5-groove pintuck foot to stitch lightweight heirloom fabrics.

- Thread the machine with a 60 wt. cotton thread.

  - Thread the top of the machine with two threads, positioning the spools so one unwinds from the top and the other from the bottom to help prevent twisting and tangling. Thread them through the machine as if they were a single thread, separating them at the needles and inserting one through each needle. Refer to your instruction manual for specifics for your machine.

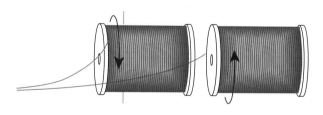

NOTE *from* NANCY

Pintucks may be accomplished using your serger. Simply serge narrow rows of 3-thread rolled edges about ¾" apart. Some sergers may require a pintuck or rolled edge foot for best results. Check your owner's manual.

- Thread the bobbin with a single lightweight thread, such as Madeira Bobbinfil thread. The bobbin thread moves back and forth on the wrong side of the fabric between the two needle threads.

- Tighten the top tension by one or two numbers or notches. This helps make the pintuck stand up and makes pintucks more predominant.

- Use a stitch length of 2.5mm–3.0mm for best results.

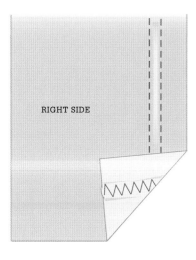

RIGHT SIDE

3 Stitch the pintucks.

- Mark the position for the first row of pintucks with an air-soluble fabric marking pen or pencil. Or pull a vertical thread and use that to position the pintucks on the precise straight of grain if using heirloom fabrics such as batiste or linen.

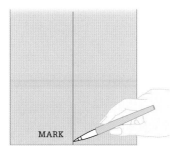

MARK

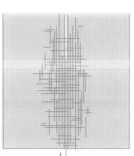

PULL A THREAD

- Stitch along the marked line. Stitch a little slower than usual because you're using two threads. Stitch accurately! If this first pintuck is straight, all subsequent tucks will also be straight.

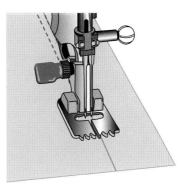

- At the end of the first pintuck, flip the fabric around without cutting threads. Place the first stitched pintuck in one of the grooves on the foot, and stitch another pintuck. (You'll be stitching in the opposite direction of the first row of stitching.) The groove selected determines the distance between pintucks.

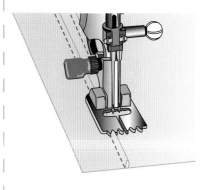

- Repeat until all of the pintucks have been stitched. Take your time to ensure that the pintuck rows are perfectly aligned.

Contrasting piping included within a seam definitely catches your eye! The contrast of colors and the narrow accents give a touch of class to a sewing or quilting project.

P

Stitched Piping

1 Cut bias strips (page 18).
- Cut strips 1¼" (32mm) wide if the pattern includes ¼" (6mm) seams.
- Cut the strips 1¾" (45mm) wide if the pattern uses ⅝" (16mm) seams.

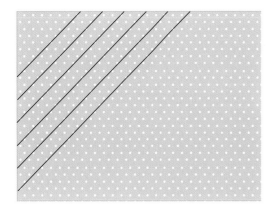

2 Prepare the piping.
- Fold the bias strips in half, wrong sides together.
- Sandwich cording in the fold of the fabric.

NOTE from NANCY

If you don't have a cording foot, a zipper foot is a good alternative. Position the needle at the left edge of the foot and stitch along the cording.

- Replace the conventional presser foot with a cording foot. Place the fabric/cording under the foot in the foot's groove. The hollowed-out section on the underside of the foot allows the cording to easily pass under the foot.

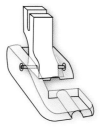

CORDING FOOT

- Adjust the sewing machine needle position so it stitches next to the cording. Stitch, matching cut edges.

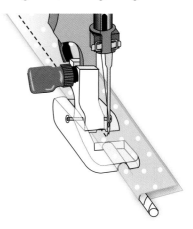

- If necessary, trim the cording seam allowance to equal the pattern's ¼" (6mm) or ⅝" (16mm) seam allowance.

EQUAL TO SEAM ALLOWANCE

3 Insert the piping into the seam.

- Sandwich the piping between two layers of fabric, right sides together, meeting the cut edges.

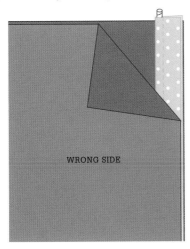

- Use a cording foot or zipper foot to stitch the seam allowance, joining the two outer sections.

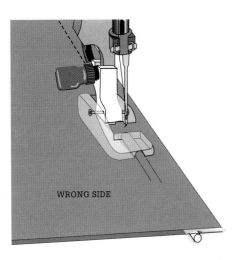

Fused Piping

1 Prepare the fabric and fuse the piping.

- Cut bias strips 1½" (38mm) wide for ¼" (6mm) seam allowances and 2" (51mm) for ⅝" (16mm) seam allowances. Using slightly wider seam allowances makes it easier to fuse the bias without getting fusible web on the underside of the iron.

- Use fusible piping. With fusible piping, the cording is sandwiched within a strip of fusible web, making it easy to position and secure.

- Fold the bias strip in half, wrong sides together, sandwiching the cording in the fold of the fabric. Be sure that the fusible web on the piping is covered by fabric.

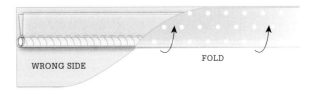

- Use the tip of an iron or a Mini Iron to secure the cording. Guide the edge of the iron along the cording, making sure you don't get web on the underside of the iron.

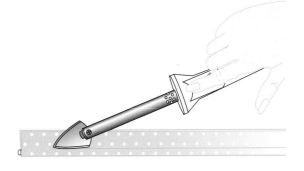

- If needed, trim the seam allowance to size.

- When inserting the piping into the seam, use a cording foot or a zipper foot. Adjust the needle position so it stitches next to the piping.

continued on next page >

2 Insert the piping into the seam.

- Place the cut edges of the piping along the edge of one layer of fabric, right sides together. Pin if necessary, placing pins perpendicular to the cut edges.

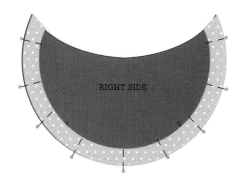

RIGHT SIDE

- Meet the right sides, sandwiching the piping between layers.

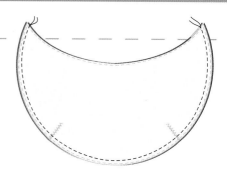

- Using a cording foot or zipper foot and the pattern seam allowance, join the two outer sections.
- Turn the project right-side-out.

Pivoting

The technique used to turn corners is called pivoting. No more starting and stopping—just stop with your needle in the down position, turn the fabric and keep on stitching!

1 Stitch to the corner. Stop with the needle down in the fabric. Lift the presser foot.

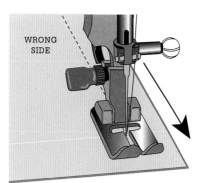

WRONG SIDE

STOP STITCHING AT CORNER; LIFT FOOT WITH NEEDLE DOWN

2 Turn the fabric so the foot lines up with the next stitching line.

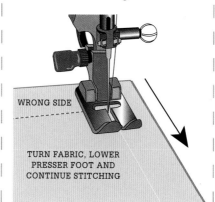

WRONG SIDE

TURN FABRIC, LOWER PRESSER FOOT AND CONTINUE STITCHING

3 Lower the presser foot and continue stitching.

NOTE from NANCY

Commercial patterns or instructions often tell you to pivot at corners. Stitching a wrapped corner seam usually gives better results. See pages 128–129 for details.

Think of a pleat as a mini-dart with no point at the end. It's easy to stitch pleats using the same techniques as those used for darts.

1 Mark pleats using short ⅛" (3mm) nips at the ends and fabric marking pen dots at the tips.

2 Pin the pleats with right sides together, matching the nips and dots.

MARK PLEATS WITH NIPS AT ENDS; PEN DOTS AT TIPS

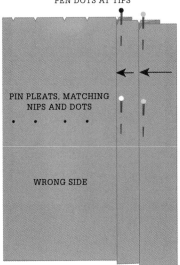

PIN PLEATS, MATCHING NIPS AND DOTS

WRONG SIDE

3 Some pleats are stitched for several inches, while others may only be secured in a seam at the upper edge.

- For stitched pleats, position the edge of a piece of cardboard between the nips and dots. Lock the stitches at the top of the pleat and stitch along the cardboard edge.

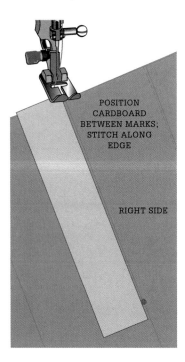

POSITION CARDBOARD BETWEEN MARKS; STITCH ALONG EDGE

RIGHT SIDE

4 Press the pleat underlays toward the side seams. This is the opposite of pressing darts, but gives a more attractive appearance.

PRESS PLEATS TOWARDS SIDES

RIGHT SIDE

WRONG SIDE

STITCH FOLD FROM UNDERSIDE

NOTE *from* NANCY

To keep the underlay of the pleat even, stitch the fold from the underside of the pleat.

P

Pocket flap seams are usually positioned at the outer edges. That sometimes results in undesirable bulk. Relocate those seams the next time you're making pocket flaps to achieve terrific results.

1 Modify the pattern.

- Place the flap pattern on a piece of tissue or pattern tracing paper.

- Machine stitch the pattern to the paper along each side seam.

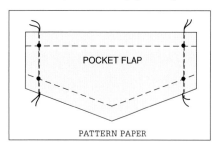

PATTERN PAPER

- Trim the paper to the same size as the original pattern. On one of the layers, mark a new vertical seam, offsetting the seam away from the side seam and center of the flap.

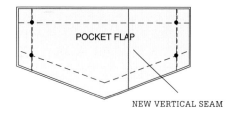

NEW VERTICAL SEAM

- Cut along the vertical line and open the pattern. Tape ⅝" (16mm) seam allowances to each side of the modified pattern.

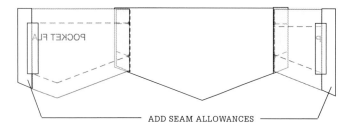

ADD SEAM ALLOWANCES

2 Stitch the pocket flap.

- Use the modified pattern to cut out the pocket flaps and fusible interfacing.

- Fuse the interfacing to the wrong side of the pocket flaps.

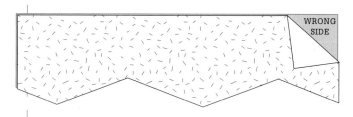

WRONG SIDE

- Stitch the vertical seam, right sides together. Press seam allowances flat, then open. Trim the seams, angle-cutting the seam ends.

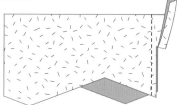

- Refold the flap, aligning the lower edges. Stitch the lower edge.

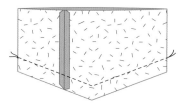

- Grade the seam, trimming the seamed portion the narrowest.

- Turn the flap right side out. Attach the pocket flap to the project following the pattern instructions.

RIGHT SIDE

Q

To meet a smaller section of fabric to a larger area, quarter marking each section provides even distribution when gathering, attaching elastic or applying ribbing. The illustrations below feature quarter marking on ribbing and a corresponding neckline.

1 Quarter the ribbing.

- Fold the ribbing in half, meeting the cut edges.

- Place a pin at the stitched seam; use it as one of the quarter marks. Place another pin at the opposite folded edge.

- Meet the two pins. Place additional pins at the two folded edges.

2 Quarter the garment neckline.

- Meet the two front shoulder seams; mark the center front. Repeat, meeting the two back shoulder seams. Mark the center back.

- Refold the neckline, meeting the pin marks. Place pins at the folds. See *Ribbing* (pages 94–95) for additional information.

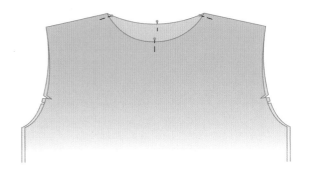

Q

Quartering and pressing a quilt block into fourths is a great way to center an appliqué. The example below features a Dresden appliqué.

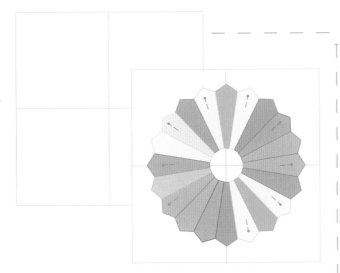

1 Quarter mark the background blocks.

- Fold the blocks in half, matching the cut edges.

- Lightly press.

- Fold the blocks in half in the opposite direction, matching the cut edges.

- Lightly press.

2 Pin the appliqué to the background square, centering it along the press marks.

Q

Make quarter-square triangles by taking two half-square triangle blocks, joining them with right sides together and cutting them in half diagonally between stitching lines.

1 Select two contrasting fabrics, one dark and one light, for each square. Fabrics may vary, depending on the combination desired for the quarter-square triangles.

2 Determine the finished size for the quarter-square triangles. Add 1¼" (32mm) to the finished dimension and cut two contrasting squares.

- For example, for a 3" (8cm) finished square, cut two 4¼" (11cm) fabric squares.

3 Use one dark and one light square to make two half-square triangles (page 52).

- Place a light and a dark square right sides together.

- Mark a diagonal line from one corner to the opposite corner, and mark ¼" (6mm) seam allowances on each side of the diagonal line.

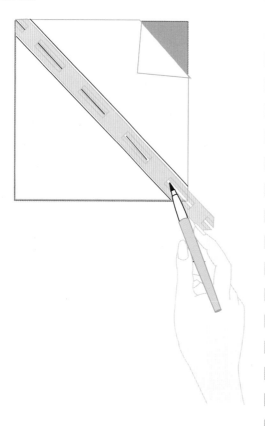

- Stitch on each of the marked seam allowance lines.

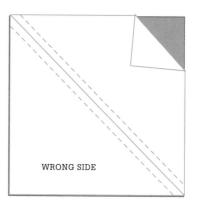

WRONG SIDE

- Cut the squares apart on the diagonal line between the seam allowances.

WRONG SIDE

4 Join the half-square triangle blocks to make quarter-squares.

• Place two half-square triangle blocks, right sides together, following the illustration below for placement. (Meet opposite colors on the two blocks.)

• Mark a diagonal line from one corner to the opposite corner, and mark ¼" (6mm) seam allowances on each side of the diagonal line. Use a Quick Quarter, if desired (page 52).

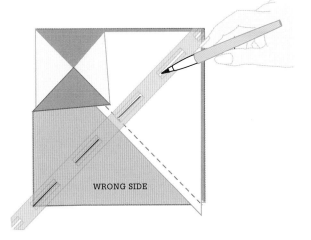

WRONG SIDE

• Stitch on each of the marked seam allowance lines.

• Cut the squares apart on the diagonal line between the seam allowances, forming two quarter-square triangle blocks.

• Press seam allowances to one side.

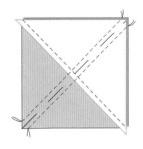
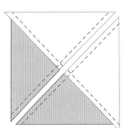
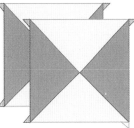

NOTE *from* **NANCY**

Whenever combining multiple solid squares with half- or quarter-square triangles to create a design, chain stitch them together to simplify construction (page 33).

Q

There are several quilting options. Among them are hand quilting, tying and various methods of machine quilting. Especially for beginners, machine quilting and tying are the fastest and easiest options.

Stitch in the Ditch

Stitching in the ditch follows the seamlines (blocks, borders, sashing, etc.) in a design. You have an easy guide to follow as you stitch.

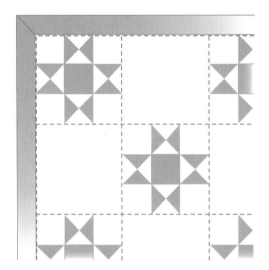

NOTE *from* NANCY

NOTE *from* NANCY

Before machine quilting any project, make sure your sewing machine is in good repair, is clean and has the tension adjusted. Always quilt from the center to the outside of your quilt to avoid shifting and bunching. Layering and pinning (pages 62–63) is the very first step for any of the quilting methods.

1 Adjust the sewing machine for machine quilting.

- Use a medium-length straight stitch with a balanced tension.

- Thread the top of the machine with cotton thread matched to the fabric, or use a monofilament thread. Available in clear and smoke colorations, monofilament thread blends with a wide variety of fabric colorations, making thread changes unnecessary.

- Insert a machine quilting needle.

- If possible, adjust the machine to stop with the needle in the down position.

- Use a walking foot to feed fabric evenly. It's important to prevent the layers of the quilt sandwich from shifting, and a walking foot helps feed all the layers through the machine smoothly and evenly.

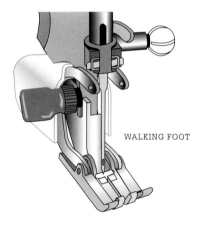

WALKING FOOT

2 Machine-quilt by stitching in the well of the seamlines with matching or monofilament thread so that stitches are less conspicuous.

- Stitch around each pieced block.

- Stitch along the border seams.

Echo Quilting

Echo quilting follows the contour of one or more of the elements of the quilt design. It helps add depth and dimension to a project.

1 Adjust the machine as detailed on page 88.

2 Machine-quilt, stitching about ¼" (6mm) from the pieced or appliquéd design.

3 Continue to echo that stitching in ¼" (6mm) increments that move outward.

NOTE *from* NANCY

Use your presser foot to help achieve uniformly spaced rows of stitching. After completing one row of stitching, guide the edge of the presser foot along the previous row of stitching.

Grid Line Quilting

Grid line quilting is uniformly spaced throughout the project. It's almost like stitching a checkerboard.

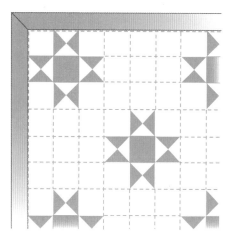

1 Adjust the machine as indicated on page 88. Use a quilting guide bar with the walking foot to keep rows of stitching an equal distance apart. Follow the instructions that came with the foot for attaching the walking foot and guide bar.

2 Machine-quilt in straight lines, both vertically and horizontally, forming a grid.

- Work from the center toward the outer edges.

- You may want to mark your quilting lines with a removable fabric pen or pencil, such as a mechanical marking pencil, to keep the rows even, if you are not using a quilting guide bar.

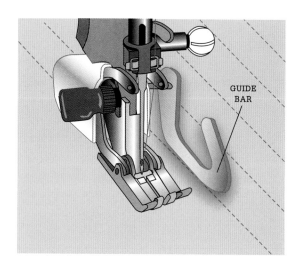

GUIDE BAR

NOTE *from* NANCY

Adjust the quilting guide bar for the width of the grid you plan to stitch. After stitching the first row, guide the bar along the previous row of stitching.

NOTE *from* NANCY

The lead in ultra-fine-point mechanical pencils intended for marking fabric isn't lead at all—it's compressed chalk. Markings can be easily and completely removed using the eraser and bristled pen end.

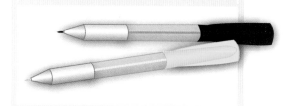

Stencil Quilting

Commercially available stencils can provide stitching guides for machine quilting designs. Some stencils are made of plastic or Templar; transfer those designs to the quilt with a fabric marker. Other machine quilting designs are printed onto paper.

1 Adjust the machine as indicated on page 88.

2 When using a commercial plastic stencil, transfer the stencil design to the project with a fabric marking pen or pencil, or with chalk and a pounce. Machine quilt following the traced design.

3 If you have drawn your own stencil, traced a design onto paper or selected a preprinted paper stencil, stitch the motif through the paper following the outline design.

- Hold the paper in position on the project by using a temporary quilt basting spray. No pins or basting stitches are required, yet the paper can be repositioned before sewing.

- Stitch directly over the paper, following the design.

- Remove the paper after stitching is completed.

NOTE *from* NANCY

Although the needle perforates the paper during machine quilting and makes removing the paper relatively easy, here's another way to simplify the process: Run the tip of a seam ripper, awl or stiletto along the stitching line, and the paper will easily separate from the stitching.

Stippling or Meandering

This technique requires free-motion stitching of small, puzzle-like designs, with the stitches never crossing or touching one another. Stippling typically refers to designs that are stitched closer together than when meandering.

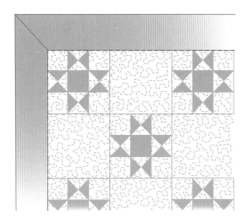

1 Set your machine up for free-motion quilting. Follow these general guidelines, but refer to your instruction manual for specifics for your machine.

- Lower or cover the feed dogs. You, rather than the feed dogs, control the motion of the fabric.

- Replace the conventional presser foot with a darning foot or Big Foot. These feet provide good surface contact with the quilt fabric and keep the fabric close to the bed of the machine. Because the feet are transparent, they allow you to clearly see where you're stitching.

- Use a cotton thread for both the bobbin and the needle, matching the color of the fabric. Or use monofilament thread in the needle and cotton or polyester thread matched to the backing in the bobbin.

- Use a machine quilting needle.

- Adjust tension as needed. If the same thread is used in both the needle and the bobbin, use a balanced tension. If the top thread is different than that in the bobbin, loosen the top tension by two numbers or notches to prevent the bobbin thread from being drawn to the top of the fabric.

BIG FOOT   DARNING FOOT

2 Stipple the quilt.

- It's not necessary to mark the design. Practice on scraps before working on your project, using the same combination of top fabric, batting and backing as in the actual project. You'll find your stippling gets better with practice.

- Position your hands on both sides of the presser foot to hold the fabrics in place and guide them during stitching. You may want to wear rubber fingers (available from an office supply store) to stabilize the fabric.

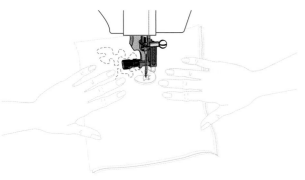

- Begin in the center of the quilt and work toward the outer edges. Stitch in small 1"–2" (3cm–5cm) sections.

- Develop a rhythm by moving the fabric slowly and stitching at a medium to fast speed.

- Remove any pins as you come to them.

- Maintain the same stitch intensity over the entire quilt surface. If some portions of the project are heavily stitched and others are lightly stitched, the finished project will not be flat or square.

Tying

Tying the quilting layers together by hand is a good choice when using a thick batting or when you would like to finish the quilting process quickly.

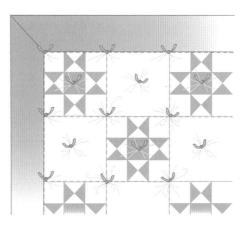

1
Select a long needle with an eye large enough to accommodate the thickness of the thread or yarn. Thread the needle with medium- to heavy-weight decorative thread, such as DMC floss or knitting yarn, in colors that coordinate or accent the patchwork design.

2
Determine the placement of the thread/yarn ties.

- Ties should be no farther apart than the width of your fist.

- Generally, the corners and centers of a patchwork pattern serve as tie placements.

3
Insert the needle through the top of the quilt, leaving a 1" (25mm) thread/yarn tail. Then, insert the needle back up through the bottom layers. Tie the thread/yarn with a square knot. Trim the yarn/thread tails to the same length.

NOTE *from* NANCY

I grew up knowing only hand-tied quilts. My aunt had a quilt frame made of four narrow boards that fit over the backs of four kitchen chairs and were held in place with clamps. In an afternoon, my relatives could easily tie two quilts while I played under the stretched quilt!

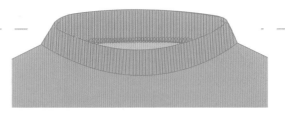

When it comes to finishing neckline edges on knit garments, an easy, traditional solution is adding a ribbed finish. Ribbing has lots of stretch—it's perfect for adding a crew neck, a mock turtleneck or a turtleneck.

R

1 Choose an appropriate fabric.

- Ribbing has 50 percent stretch or more. It gives a garment a sporty look.

- If you don't have matching ribbing, another option is to use the garment fabric, as long as the fabric has at least 50 percent stretch.

  - To determine whether the fabric has adequate stretch, use a 5" (13cm) crosswise grain section of the fabric. Stretch the fabric. If it easily stretches to at least 7½" (19cm), the fabric is suitable.

- Cut the ribbing or the garment fabric to the size that the pattern indicates.

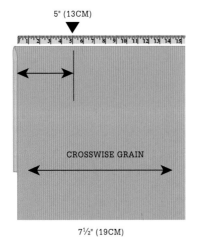

5" (13CM)

CROSSWISE GRAIN

7½" (19CM)

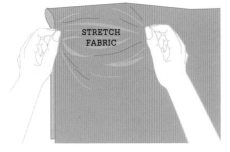

STRETCH FABRIC

2 Stitch seams.

- Stitch or serge the shoulder seams of the garment.

WRONG SIDE

- Stitch the ribbing into a circle. There is no right or wrong side, so meet the short ends and stitch a ¼" (6mm) seam. Finger press the seam open.

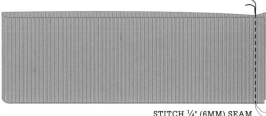

STITCH ¼" (6MM) SEAM

3 Quarter the neckline and the ribbing (page 85).

4 Stitch or serge the ribbing to the garment.

- Stitch with the garment next to the machine bed.
- Slightly stretch the ribbing to meet the neckline.

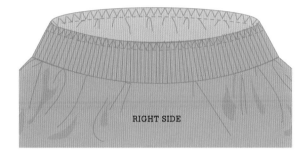

RIGHT SIDE

- To serge the seam:
  - Insert your finger under the two needle threads before they enter the needle to create some slack.
  - Remove the stitches from the stitch finger so you start serging with a clean stitch.

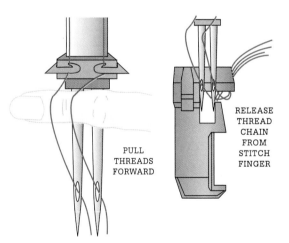

PULL THREADS FORWARD

RELEASE THREAD CHAIN FROM STITCH FINGER

- Serge around the neckline. Overstitch a few stitches when you reach the beginning point.

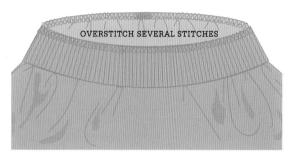

OVERSTITCH SEVERAL STITCHES

- Insert your finger under the needle threads again to create some slack; remove the threads from the stitch finger and serge off.
- Press the seam toward the garment.
- *Optional*: Topstitch on the right side of the garment ¼" (6mm) from the seam.

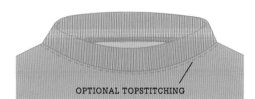

OPTIONAL TOPSTITCHING

R

You can't put your serger in reverse and simply back up to remove stitches. But here's a simple two-step reverse-serging technique that you can learn in a minute or less. Use the foot of your serger as an anchor to hold the fabric in place.

1 Anchor the serged fabric by placing it under the serger presser foot and lowering the foot.

2 Insert the tip of a seam ripper between the two pieces of fabric and under the looper threads that wrap around the seam. Carefully rip through the entire length of the seam. If the seam is long, you may need to periodically stop and reposition the presser foot.

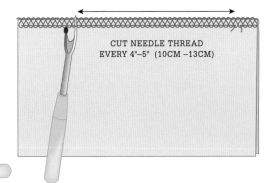

CUT NEEDLE THREAD
EVERY 4"–5" (10CM –13CM)

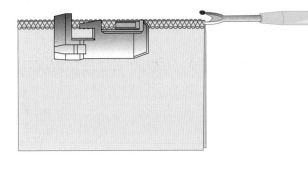

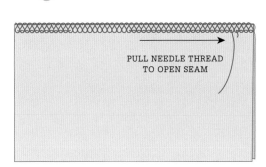

PULL NEEDLE THREAD
TO OPEN SEAM

3 If the seam is long, cut the needle thread(s) every 4"–5" (10cm –13cm) by slipping a seam ripper under the stitching.

4 Pull the needle thread (the left needle thread if using a 3-thread or 4-thread machine) and the seam will open with ease.

Ripping: STITCHED SEAMS

R

"As ye sew, so shall ye rip!" Perhaps I've taken creative license with this phrase; nevertheless, it's true. Here's the simplest way to reverse stitch.

The bobbin thread is usually the looser of the two threads in a seam. Use your seam ripper to clip through a stitch about every 2" (5cm). Pull the top thread. Presto—stitches are gone!

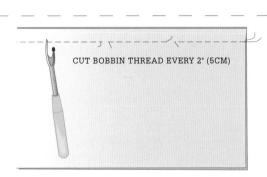

CUT BOBBIN THREAD EVERY 2" (5CM)

Using a rod pocket is one of several ways to hang a wall hanging. Although there are many different methods for making a rod pocket, this is my favorite. It's easy and fast to construct.

R

1 From the backing fabric, cut a rod pocket 6"–8" (15cm –20cm) wide and a little narrower than the top of your wall hanging.

2 Clean finish the 6"–8" (15cm –20cm) edges of the rod pocket strip by turning under ¼" (6mm) on each short edge twice. Press and stitch.

WRONG SIDE

3 Press the rod pocket in half lengthwise, wrong sides together, meeting the cut edges.

RIGHT SIDE

FOLD

4 Center the rod pocket on the back of the wall hanging, aligning the top cut edges, before adding the binding. Baste in place.

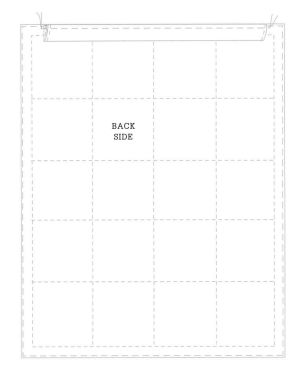

BACK
SIDE

5 Bind the edges as usual. After the binding is completed, roll back the folded edge of the rod pocket ¼"–½" (6mm –13mm), exposing the back side of the pocket. Finger press. Pin the finger-pressed fold to the backing fabric.

6 Hand-stitch along the pinned fold, catching only a single layer of fabric.

HAND-STITCH ALONG FOLD

R

Create yards of ruffles or pleats in mere minutes with a uniquely designed ruffler foot. I prefer to use this foot on mid-line to lower-line sewing machine models, rather than on computerized sewing machines. At first glance this foot appears intimidating, but don't let appearances fool you! It's just waiting to help produce even gathers and pleats while creating accents for your home or wearable art.

1 Set up your machine.

- Thread the needle and bobbin with all-purpose thread.

- Use a universal needle appropriate to the weight of the fabric.

- Attach a ruffler foot, following the package instructions.

  – Raise the needle bar to its highest position.

  – Attach the foot to the machine, placing the fork arm over the sewing machine's needle clamp screw.

- Use a straight stitch with a balanced tension. The stitch length varies, depending on the desired fullness of the ruffle.

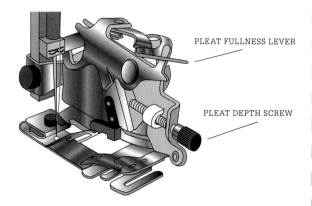

PLEAT FULLNESS LEVER

PLEAT DEPTH SCREW

2 Place the fabric under the separator guide, between the ruffling blade and the separator blades.

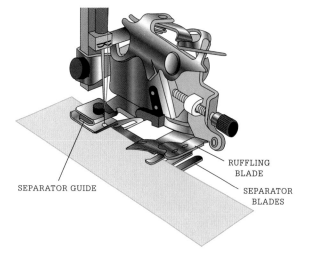

SEPARATOR GUIDE

RUFFLING BLADE

SEPARATOR BLADES

3 Stitch at an even, steady speed, gently guiding the fabric to allow the foot to feed even amounts of fabric. Allow the foot to feed the fabric—if you hold the fabric too firmly, the teeth will not form consistent pleats.

4 Make a test ruffle to ensure that the amount of fullness is what you want. If necessary, change settings and test again.

- The pleat fullness lever controls how often the ruffler makes a gather or pleat. The lever can be set to gather every stitch, every sixth stitch or every twelfth stitch, depending on the desired fullness.

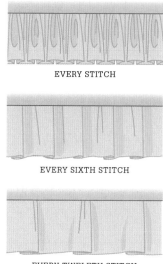

EVERY STITCH

EVERY SIXTH STITCH

EVERY TWELFTH STITCH

- The pleat depth screw regulates a spring that determines how deep each pleat is. Tighten it for deeper ruffles; loosen it for shallower ruffles.

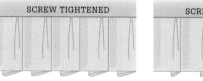

SCREW TIGHTENED

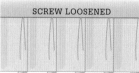

SCREW LOOSENED

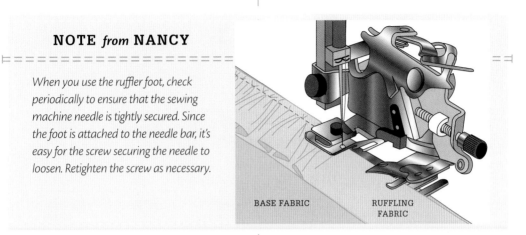

BASE FABRIC   RUFFLING FABRIC

5 Changing the stitch length also affects the amount of fullness in the ruffle. If all other settings are similar, the shorter the stitch length, the fuller the ruffle.

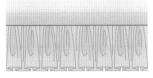

SHORTER STITCH LENGTH   LONGER STITCH LENGTH

6 Seam ruffle strips together.

- For a single layer ruffle, hem the outer edge of the ruffle.

- If necessary, clean finish the seam allowances.

- To make a double ruffle, meet lengthwise edges of ruffle and machine-baste the cut edges together.

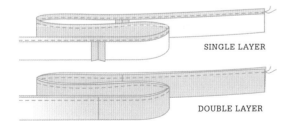

SINGLE LAYER

DOUBLE LAYER

Making and Attaching Ruffles at the Same Time

Next, make that ruffler foot go a step further. When you want to add a ruffle to a project—for example, a pillow or a dust ruffle—it's possible to prepare the ruffle and attach it all in one step. That's a real time and energy saver!

1 Prepare the ruffle.

- Measure the length of the area to which the ruffle will be applied. Multiply by 2.5 or 3.0, depending on the amount of fullness desired. It's best to allow slightly more fabric than needed, since the ruffle fullness cannot be adjusted once it is attached.

- Prepare a single or double ruffle, as indicated at left, allowing for seam allowances.

2 Set up the machine as detailed previously.

3 Place the fabric under the separator guide, then between the ruffling blade and the separator blades.

4 Place the fabric to which the ruffle will be attached under the separator guide, then between the separator blade and the feed dogs.

5 Lower the presser bar and stitch. The ruffle is gathered and attached simultaneously.

S

Most woven fabrics ravel unless the edges are finished. After stitching a seam, add a seam finish to each seam edge to prevent fraying. Most seam finishes are done on a single thickness of fabric to avoid bulk and make the seam flatter and neater. Here are several ways to finish seams.

Zigzag Each Seam Edge

- Use a medium-width zigzag and a medium to short stitch length.

- Stitch the zig in the fabric and the zag close to or off the cut edge.

- Zigzagging works best on medium- to heavy-weight fabrics. If zigzagging draws in the seam edge and makes it pucker, you may want to choose another seam finish.

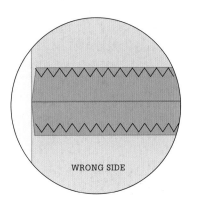

WRONG SIDE

Serge Each Seam Edge

- Use a 3-thread or 4-thread serged overlock stitch (pages 108–109).

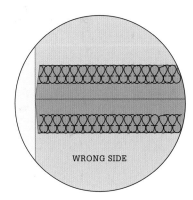

WRONG SIDE

NOTE *from* NANCY

Edgestitching close to the seam edge is my least favorite option for seam finishing. However, this method may be your only choice if you don't own a serger and your machine has problems stitching a zigzag so close to the fabric edge.

Edgestitch Close to Each Seam Edge

- Set the machine to straight stitch.

- Guide the right edge of the presser foot along the cut edge of the fabric.

- You may want to adjust the needle position so it's closer to the fabric edge. (Stitching is about ⅛"–¼" [3mm–6mm] from the cut edge.)

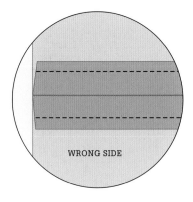

WRONG SIDE

NOTE *from* NANCY

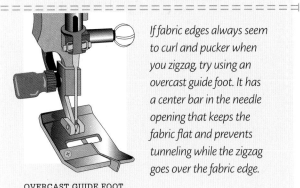

If fabric edges always seem to curl and pucker when you zigzag, try using an overcast guide foot. It has a center bar in the needle opening that keeps the fabric flat and prevents tunneling while the zigzag goes over the fabric edge.

OVERCAST GUIDE FOOT

For very sheer fabrics or fabrics that ravel easily, French seams enclose the seam allowances, giving a neat finish that practically eliminates ravelling. French seams are a perfect choice for joining fabrics such as batiste, chiffon and voile. With two rows of straight stitching and a little pressing, you can encase the raw edges of the fabric attractively and neatly.

1 Place wrong sides together with the raw edges aligned. Straight stitch ⅜" (10mm) from the cut edges.

2 Trim the seam allowance to just slightly less than ¼" (6mm) using a rotary cutter and cutting mat.

3 Press the joined edges flat and then press the seam open.

- This makes it easier to fold the seam allowance along the first stitching line in preparation for the second row of machine stitching.

4 Refold the seam allowance with the right sides of the fabric together, positioning the first stitching line at the fold. To complete the French seam, stitch ¼" (6mm) from the fold, encasing the cut edges.

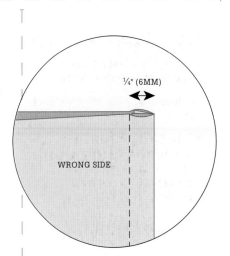

¼" (6MM)

WRONG SIDE

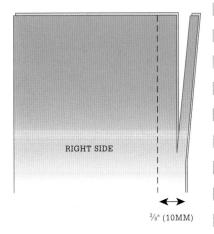

RIGHT SIDE

⅜" (10MM)

NOTE *from* NANCY

To save time, I often reverse the width of the seam allowances, stitching the ¼" (6mm) seam first, then the ⅜" (10mm) seam. This method produces a slightly wider seam, but it eliminates the trimming step. For extremely sheer fabric, the narrower width is best.

For most projects on medium-weight woven fabric, traditional seams work well for joining the fabric edges.

1 Set the sewing machine to stitch 10–12 stitches per inch (per 2.5cm).

2 Place the right sides of two pieces of fabric together, matching the seam edges, the top and bottom of the pieces, and the notches.

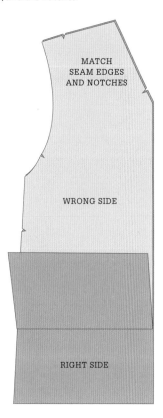

MATCH
SEAM EDGES
AND NOTCHES

WRONG SIDE

RIGHT SIDE

3 Pin the edges together, placing the pins at right angles to the edge of the fabric.

4 Stitch the seam.

- Check the pattern's seam allowance. Most patterns allow ⅝" (16mm) but some allow only ¼" (6mm). It is important to stitch exactly on the seamline.

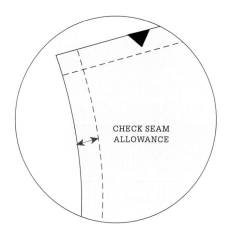

CHECK SEAM
ALLOWANCE

- Make sure the upper and bobbin threads are at the back of the machine, under the presser foot.

- Place the end of the seam under the presser foot. Lower the presser foot.

- Lower the needle into the fabric by turning the balance wheel.

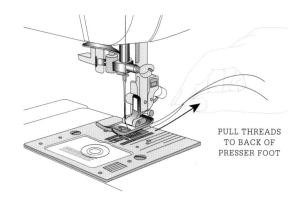

PULL THREADS
TO BACK OF
PRESSER FOOT

- Lock the stitches at the beginning and end of each seam to prevent them from coming out: Sew two or three stitches, then adjust the machine to stitch in reverse and sew two or three stitches—this is backstitching.

- Adjust the machine to stitch forward again and continue stitching. Guide the fabric so the seam is a uniform width.

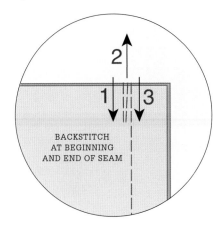

BACKSTITCH
AT BEGINNING
AND END OF SEAM

- Remove each pin as you come to it.

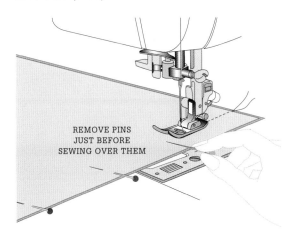

REMOVE PINS
JUST BEFORE
SEWING OVER THEM

- Stitch to the seam end and backstitch.

- Turn the balance wheel until the take-up lever is at its highest point.

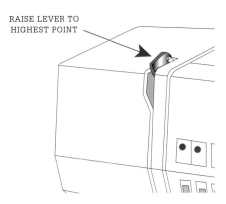

RAISE LEVER TO
HIGHEST POINT

- Raise the presser bar lifter and pull the fabric to the back of the machine under the presser foot.

- Cut the threads close to the fabric. Leave 2"–3" (5cm–8cm) of thread coming from the machine needle.

- Trim the thread ends at the beginning of the seam close to the fabric.

NOTE *from* NANCY

Another way to lock stitch is to stitch in place several times. Set the stitch length lever at 0 and make two to three stitches. Then return the stitch length to 10–12 stitches per inch (per 2.5cm) and continue stitching. Repeat this at the end of the seam.

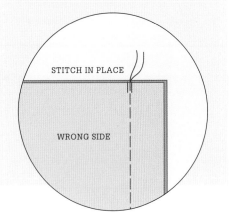

STITCH IN PLACE

WRONG SIDE

S

Eliminate all but one of the cover stitch needles and you'll have a chain stitch. Some sergers are set up so the left needle stitches a ⅝" (16mm) seam allowance, the middle needle a ½" (13mm) seam allowance, and the right needle a ⅜" (10mm) seam allowance. From the top side, it looks like a regular machine stitch, but the back of the stitch forms loops. If you pull the correct thread, the stitches all come out as you pull.

Serger Setup for a Chain Stitch

- **Presser Foot:** Regular
- **Needles:** Left, Center or Right
- **Throat Plate:** Normal
- **Stitch Length:** 2mm to 3mm
- **Differential Feed:** Normal
- **Blade Position:** Down
- **Needle Tension:** 4–6
- **Chain Looper Tension:** Normal
- **Lower Looper Tension:** Chain/Normal
- Add Stitch Table
- Disengage Upper Looper

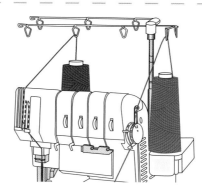

Seaming with a Chain Stitch

- With right sides together, place the fabric under the needle.
- Line up the edge of the fabric with the edge of the needle plate.
- Serge the seam.

Topstitching with a Chain Stitch

- Lengthen your stitch length for topstitching.
- Place the edge of the fabric under the needle and start to serge. Use two strands of all-purpose thread in the needle for a heavier look to the topstitching.

S

Use the left and right needles along with the chain looper to produce the widest cover stitch. This stitch is used widely in the ready-to-wear industry for hemming knit and woven garments. It is generally used with the double stitch on the right side, but in other instances the chain looper adds a charming accent to the right side of a garment.

NOTE *from* NANCY

You need to have a machine that is a combination overlock/cover-lock/chain stitch serger or a cover stitch/chain stitch serger to utilize these stitches. Check your instruction manual to see if your serger is capable of serging a cover stitch.

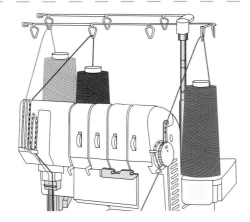

- Kiss an anchor cloth to the line of cover stitching.

- Chain off onto the anchor cloth. This prevents stitch jams under the presser foot. On some cover stitch machines, this is not necessary or it only needs to be done at initial setup. Check your instruction manual.

Serger Setup for a Cover Stitch

- **Presser Foot:** Regular

- **Needles:** Left and Right

- **Throat Plate:** Normal

- **Stitch Length:** 3mm to 4mm

- **Differential Feed:** Normal

- **Blade Position:** Down

- **Left or Right Needle Tension:** 4–6

- **Chain Looper Tension:** Cover/Normal

- Add Stitch Table

- Disengage Upper Looper

Serging a Cover Stitch

- Thread and prepare the machine following the instruction manual.

- Place the fabric under the presser foot, directly below the needles.

- Start to serge slowly. All basic overlock machines are able to stitch without fabric underneath the presser foot. However, when serging a cover stitch, it's advisable to start stitching directly on fabric and to use an anchor cloth (page 7) at the end of the line of stitching. Again, check your instruction manual for recommendations.

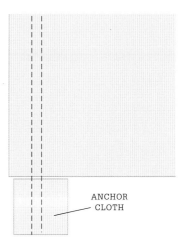

ANCHOR CLOTH

NOTE *from* NANCY

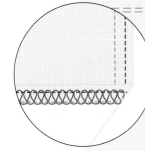

Use the center and right needles or the center and left needles with the chain looper to produce a narrow cover stitch. This stitch simulates a double-needle stitch on top of the fabric.

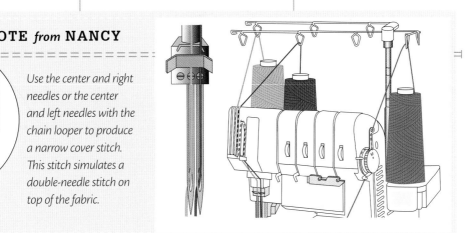

Flatlock is an overlock method that forms a seam that, when pulled, lies flat on the surface of the fabric. This stitch can be functional or used as a decorative accent on numerous garments or crafts. Embellishing creative projects is its forte, but it is also a very stretchy, durable seam to use on activewear and lingerie.

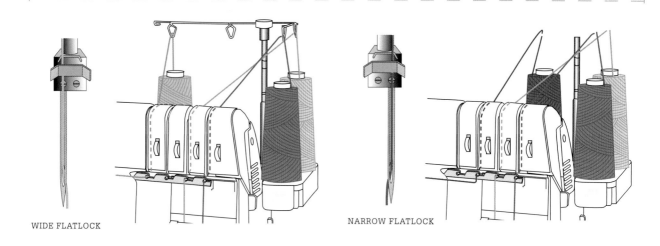

WIDE FLATLOCK

NARROW FLATLOCK

Setup for a 3-Thread Flatlock Stitch—Wide or Narrow

- **Presser Foot:** Regular
- **Needles:** Left or Right
- **Throat Plate:** Normal
- **Stitch Width:** Wide/Normal
- **Stitch Length:** 1mm to 3mm
- **Differential Feed:** Normal
- **Blade Position:** Down
- **Left or Right Needle Tension:** Loosen
- **Upper Looper Tension:** Tighten
- **Lower Looper Tension:** Tighten

3-Thread Flatlock Stitch—Wide or Narrow

- Use the right needle for a narrow flatlock and the left needle for a wide flatlock.

- Choose coordinating or contrasting decorative threads for an elegant look. Don't underestimate the ease and versatility of this serging option.

- Serge a seam or the fold of a fabric; pull the two layers apart until the serging lies flat.

NOTE *from* NANCY

The key to a perfect flatlock is eliminating the needle tension. To do this, I remove the thread from the tension disc and then tighten the needle tension completely. The thread will ride over the disc with virtually no tension on the needle thread.

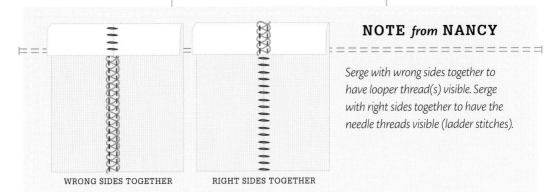

WRONG SIDES TOGETHER　　　RIGHT SIDES TOGETHER

NOTE *from* NANCY

Serge with wrong sides together to have looper thread(s) visible. Serge with right sides together to have the needle threads visible (ladder stitches).

Flatlock a Seam

- Position the cut edges about ⅛" (3mm) away from the blade. Serge so the loops form slightly beyond the cut edges. Do not trim away any of the fabric.

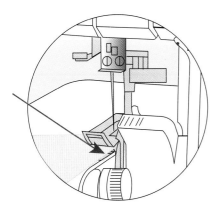

- Serge to the end of the seam, clearing the stitch finger. Then chain off the fabric for 3"–4" (8cm–10cm).

- Pull the fabric layers apart until the stitches lie flat.

Flatlock within a Project

- Fold the fabric at the desired position.

- Place the folded edge approximately ⅛" (3mm) away from the blade so the stitches form off the edge of the fabric. This makes it easy to flatten out the fabric after flatlocking is completed.

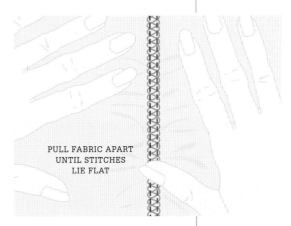

PULL FABRIC APART
UNTIL STITCHES
LIE FLAT

NOTE *from* NANCY

A 2-thread flatlock is another flatlock option on some sergers. It uses less thread and is less bulky for overedging heavier weight fabrics. Check your manual to make sure your serger is able to stitch with two threads; not all models have this feature. Your serger must have a 2-thread converter (a spring that closes the eye of the upper looper) to achieve this stitch.

S

The 4-thread overlock is the most basic stitch on a serger. It is strong and reinforced—a perfect stitch on denim—yet it can be used on stretch fabrics because it has a fair amount of give. This stitch uses two needles plus the upper and lower loopers; hence, the name 4-thread overlock. On most sergers, the left needle in a 4-thread stitch is ¼" (6mm) from the cutting blade.

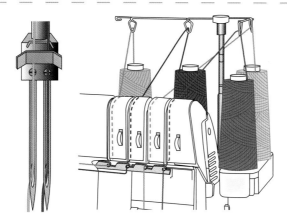

Serger Setup for a 4-Thread Overlock Stitch

- **Presser Foot:** Regular
- **Needles:** Left and Right
- **Throat Plate:** Normal
- **Stitch Width:** Normal to Wide
- **Stitch Length:** 2.5mm to 3.5mm
- **Differential Feed:** Normal
- **Blade Position:** Up
- **Left Needle Tension:** Normal
- **Right Needle Tension:** Normal
- **Upper Looper Tension:** Normal
- **Lower Looper Tension:** Normal

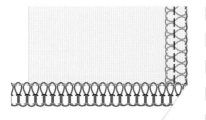

Serging a 4-Thread Overlock

- Chain off 2"–3" (5cm–8cm) of thread.

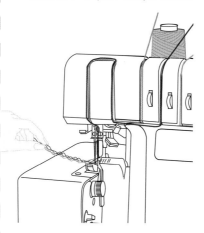

- Start to feed fabric under the presser foot. It is not necessary to completely lift the presser foot. Many sergers have a spring foot. Slightly lift the front of the foot to get the fabric to feed.

- Position the fabric.
  - With ⅝" (16mm) seam allowances, use the ⅝" (16mm) seam guide. The seam will be trimmed to ¼" (6mm) as you serge.

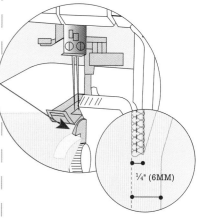

¼" (6MM)

⅝" (16MM)

  - With ¼" (6mm) seam allowances, guide fabric to the left of the cutting blade.

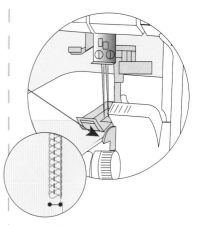

¼" (6MM)

The 3-thread overlock stitch has more stretch built into it than the 4-thread overlock and also conserves thread. Use it on seams that don't require the extra stability of the second needle thread. You will have one needle thread and two looper threads (upper and lower) overcasting the edges. To obtain a narrow 3-thread stitch, use the right needle. For a wide 3-thread stitch, use the left needle.

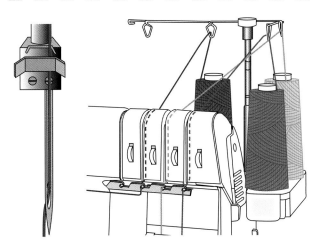

NOTE *from* NANCY

Whenever you remove or replace a needle, remember to securely tighten the needle clamp screw. Otherwise, the vibration created as you serge may cause the screw to loosen and come flying off.

Serger Setup for a 3-Thread Overlock Stitch

- **Presser Foot:** Regular
- **Needles:** Right or Left (depending on seam width)
- **Throat Plate:** Normal
- **Stitch Width:** Narrow to Normal
- **Stitch Length:** 2.5mm to 3.5mm
- **Differential Feed:** Normal
- **Blade Position:** Up
- **Right Needle Tension:** Normal
- **Upper Looper Tension:** Normal
- **Lower Looper Tension:** Normal

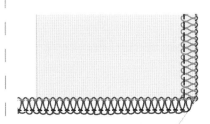

Serging a 3-Thread Overlock

- Seaming knits: The 3-thread overlock provides durability and stretch for seaming light- to medium-weight stretchy knits such as lingerie, swimwear and interlock. Use Woolly Nylon Thread in the needle and loopers for extra stretch and softness.

- Overcasting seams with a 3-thread overlock keeps them from raveling, gives a neat finished look to the project and doesn't add bulk.

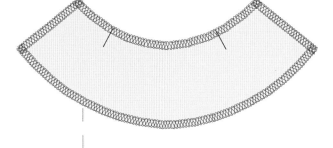

S

Rolled-edge hemming is especially attractive on table linens, but it is also suitable for seaming sheer and lightweight fabrics. For a common 3-thread rolled edge, the upper looper thread wraps around the edge of the fabric, and the lower looper forms almost a straight line of stitching on the back of the fabric.

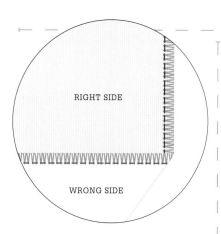

RIGHT SIDE

WRONG SIDE

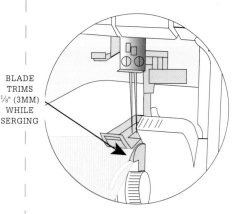

• **Blade Position:** Up or Unlocked so you can trim off about ⅛" (3mm) of the fabric while serging.

BLADE TRIMS ⅛" (3MM) WHILE SERGING

Thread Options for Serging Rolled Edges

• Regular 2-ply cone thread (needle, upper looper and lower looper)

• Rayon thread (needle, upper looper and lower looper)

• Woolly Nylon Thread (upper looper and lower looper; regular serger cone thread in needle)

• Metallic (upper looper; regular serger cone thread in the needle and Woolly Nylon in the lower looper)

• Fine yarn, such as Polyarn (texturized polyester) thread (upper looper; regular serger cone thread in needle and lower looper or use Woolly Nylon in the lower looper)

Serger Setup for a 3-Thread Rolled Edge

• **Presser Foot:** Rolled Edge (Change presser foot if specified in the instruction manual. Some sergers require a rolled edge foot with a narrow stitch finger.)

• **Needles:** Right needle only

• **Throat Plate:** Some sergers require a special throat plate to do rolled hemming. Check your instruction manual.

• **Stitch Width:** Narrow to Normal

• **Stitch Length:** 1mm to 2mm (Some machines have a special stitch length adjustment for a rolled edge, often marked with an *R*.)

• **Differential Feed:** Normal

• **Right Needle Tension:** Loosen

• **Lower Looper Tension:** Tighten lower looper tension almost completely.

Note: Check your instruction manual for your serger specifications.

LOOSEN RIGHT NEEDLE TENSION

TIGHTEN LOWER LOOPER TENSION

NOTE *from* NANCY

Use Woolly Nylon Thread in the lower looper when you need a tighter tension for a rolled edge. This specialty thread contracts and pulls the upper looper thread around the edge. You will achieve tight, smooth rolled hems.

You can also use Woolly Nylon in the needle in addition to the loopers for soft knit edges. To make threading easier, put a drop of seam sealant such a Fray Block or Fray Check on the tip of your finger and roll the needle thread end between your finger and thumb. Let dry and trim at an angle, if necessary.

S

The lettuce edge is a variation of the rolled edge. Stretch the fabric edge in front of and behind the presser foot as you serge. When you release the fabric after stitching, you will have a curled look. It works great on knit ribbed necklines and cuffs, as well as hems on lightweight knit shirts and trim on Lycra swimsuits and activewear.

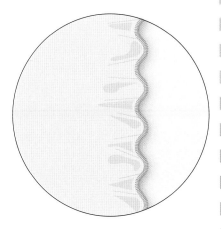

Serger Setup for a Lettuce Edge

- Use Woolly Nylon Thread in the loopers and regular cone thread in the needle for an attractive lettuce edge.

- Use a normal width and a rolled hem length setting of 1–2.

- Lock or disengage the cutting blade, if possible.

- Lower the differential feed, if available, to about 0.6.

- Guide the fabric along the right edge of the presser foot.

- Stretch the ribbing or single knit an equal amount from front and back while serging.

- Serge at a slow to moderate speed.

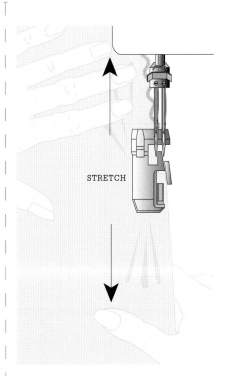

STRETCH

NOTE *from* NANCY

Try the lettuce edge on a ready-made t-shirt neckline, hem or sleeve cuffs to add your own special touch.

S

The following are my favorite techniques to use when setting in a shirt sleeve or a cap sleeve.

General Sleeve Information

There are two general types of sleeves: a shirt sleeve and a cap sleeve. A shirt sleeve has less slope, a shorter cap and less ease than a traditional cap sleeve. A cap sleeve has a greater slope, higher cap and more ease than a shirt sleeve. It must always be eased to fit the armhole.

A sleeve generally has one notch indicating the front of the sleeve and two notches indicating the back. A circle marking indicates the position for the shoulder seam. Be sure to transfer these markings to the sleeve and the garment.

SHIRT SLEEVE

CAP SLEEVE

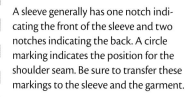

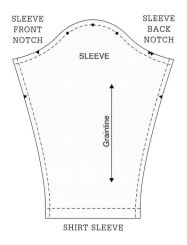

SLEEVE
FRONT
NOTCH

SLEEVE
BACK
NOTCH

SLEEVE

Grainline

SHIRT SLEEVE

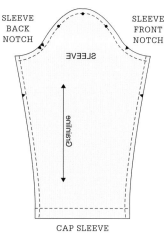

SLEEVE
BACK
NOTCH

SLEEVE
FRONT
NOTCH

SLEEVE

Grainline

CAP SLEEVE

NOTE *from* NANCY

If the right and wrong sides of your fabric look alike, mark an X on the wrong side with a marking pen or pencil, or chalk. Or place a small piece of tape on the wrong side of the fabric to prevent two left sleeves.

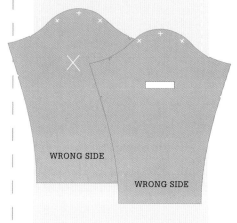

WRONG SIDE

WRONG SIDE

Shirt Sleeve Construction

Inserting a shirt sleeve is easy using this flat construction technique. The sleeve cap has a slight amount of ease. By using the sewing machine's capabilities, that fullness can be effectively eased to fit the armhole. You'll master this technique in no time flat.

1. Do not join the underarm seams of the garment or the sleeve.

2. Easing is unnecessary. Pin the sleeve to the armhole with right sides together, meeting the cut edges, shoulder positions and notches. Pin from the garment side.

3. Position the sleeve and garment at the machine so the sleeve is next to the feed dogs.

4. Stitch the sleeve in place. Press the seams flat, then toward the sleeve.

5. Stitch the underarm seam, sewing both the side seam and sleeve underarm seam. Press the seam flat, then toward the back.

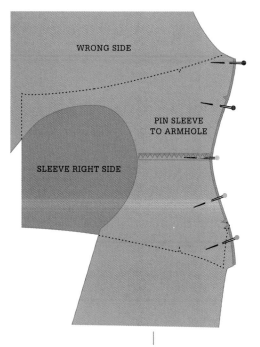

WRONG SIDE

PIN SLEEVE
TO ARMHOLE

SLEEVE RIGHT SIDE

WRONG SIDE

NOTE *from* NANCY

Whenever you join two pieces of fabric that are different lengths, always place the longer edge next to the sewing machine feed dogs. The feed dogs will ease the longer layer to meet the top layer.

Cap Sleeve Construction

Sleeve ease is essential for wearing comfort, but it's also important that the sleeve fits smoothly into the armhole. If your garment has a cap sleeve with greater slope and a higher cap, this fullness must be eased to fit the armhole.

continued on next page >

Easy Does It! Sleeve Easing

Here are two options for easing in sleeve fullness. Experiment with these choices to see which you prefer.

Option 1: Sew two rows of machine stitching

- Change the stitch length to basting, about 6 stitches per inch (per 2.5cm).

- Stitch one basting row from notch to notch, ⅝" (16mm) from the cut edge of the sleeve cap. Leave 2"–3" (5cm–8cm) thread tails at the beginning and end of the stitching.

- Stitch a second basting row from notch to notch ¼" (6mm) from the cut edge of the sleeve cap.

WRONG SIDE

- Fasten the bobbin threads at one end of the stitching by wrapping them around a pin in a figure eight.

WRONG SIDE

- At the other end of the stitching, pull both bobbin threads until the size of the sleeve matches that of the armhole.

- Fasten the threads by wrapping them around a pin in a figure eight.

FASTEN BOBBIN THREADS

WRONG SIDE

Option 2: Finger easing

This method requires only one row of stitching between notches and is perfect for light- to medium-weight fabrics. If you haven't tried this technique before, practice on a fabric scrap until you get the hang of it.

- Adjust the stitch length according to the fabric weight: 10–12 stitches per inch (per 2.5cm) for medium-weight fabrics and 12–14 stitches per inch (per 2.5cm) for lightweight.

- Stitch ½" (13mm) from the cut edge of the sleeve cap.

- Firmly press your finger against the back of the presser foot. Stitch 2"–3" (5cm–8cm), trying to stop the fabric from flowing through the machine. Release your finger and repeat. Your finger will prevent the flow of fabric from behind the presser foot, causing the feed dogs to ease each stitch slightly.

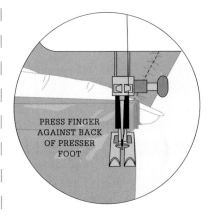

PRESS FINGER AGAINST BACK OF PRESSER FOOT

- It's important that you press very firmly. If you don't, the fabric will continue to move through the machine and the sleeve cap will not be eased. Press down hard with your finger.

- If you have eased too much, simply snip a stitch or two to release some of the gathers. If you need to gather more, pull a thread.

Use snaps to hold together edges that overlap and don't get much strain. Snaps come in several sizes, ranging from a tiny size 4/0 to a large size 4.

1 First, sew on the ball half of the snap, attaching it to the wrong side of the overlap.

- Use a single, knotted thread. Hide the knot between the fabric and the snap.

- Stitch through one hole several times, placing the stitches close together. Stitch only through the facing and the interfacing. **Do not** stitch through to the right side of the project.

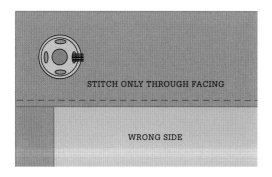

STITCH ONLY THROUGH FACING

WRONG SIDE

- After stitching one hole, insert the needle under the snap. Bring the thread out in the next hole.

- Stitch through all four holes in the same way. Knot the thread close to the fabric.

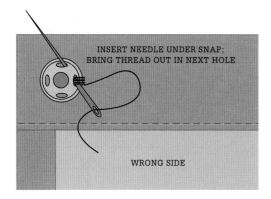

INSERT NEEDLE UNDER SNAP; BRING THREAD OUT IN NEXT HOLE

WRONG SIDE

NOTE *from* NANCY

To mark the location for the socket quickly and easily, rub a piece of chalk over the end of the ball. Position the ball over the other part of the project as if the project were closed. Finger press the two fabric layers together. The chalk will mark the position for the socket.

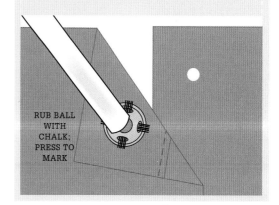

RUB BALL WITH CHALK; PRESS TO MARK

2 Position the socket half of the snap on the right side of the underlap. Stitch through the socket holes just as you stitched through holes on the ball half.

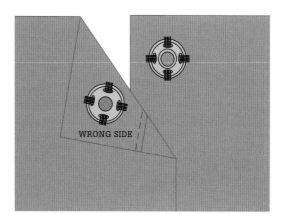

WRONG SIDE

Snaps can also hold together two edges that meet, preventing them from gaping or pulling apart. These snaps are called swing or hanging snaps.

1 Place the ball half of the snap at one edge of the opening so only one hole touches the fabric. The remainder of the ball will extend past the fabric edge.

2 Stitch the ball half to the garment, sewing through only one hole. Use a single, knotted thread.

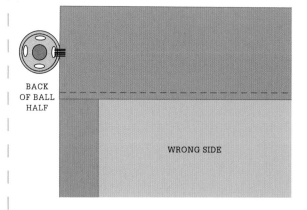

BACK
OF BALL
HALF

WRONG SIDE

3 Rub chalk on the ball. Place the two project sections so the edges of the opening just meet. Mark the position for the socket half.

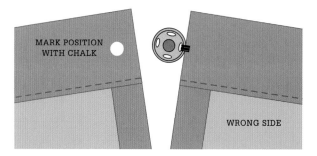

MARK POSITION
WITH CHALK

WRONG SIDE

4 Stitch through all the holes of the socket half, sewing though only the facing and interfacing.

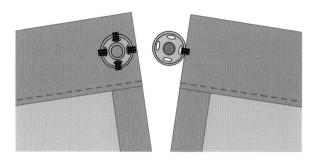

Squaring a quilted project is essential for a professional look. With quilted wall hangings, squaring also makes the project hang more evenly.

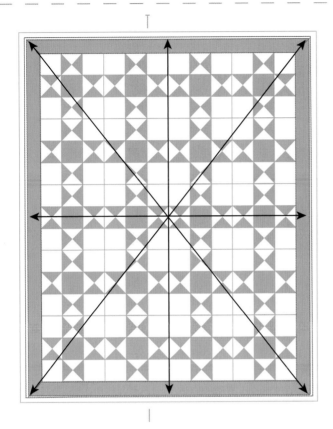

1 Measure the project from top to bottom, side to side, and corner to corner to ensure it is square.

2 Trim the edges as needed to achieve square corners and uniform measurements.

3 Clip any loose threads and give the quilt top a final pressing.

NOTE *from* NANCY

Use The Block Marker to perfectly align the sides and corners of your quilt blocks before joining the blocks. It's a must-have quilting notion!

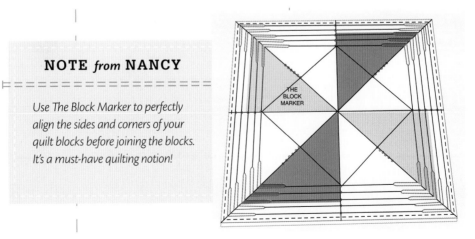

S

By definition, a stabilizer is designed to support or even replace fabric under the stress of decorative stitching and, most commonly, under computerized machine embroidery.

Stabilizers are organized into categories based on how you remove them—cut-aways, tear-aways, wash-aways and heat-away, plus a liquid-and-spray category that is usually used in conjunction with one of the other stabilizers. It's important that you take the time to test the different types! Stitching test samples will give you an accurate idea of how stabilizers will perform with your type of decorative stitching.

Cut-Aways

Cut-away stabilizers are placed on the wrong side of the fabric prior to stitching. They resist stretching and remain on your fabric for the life of the project. Cut-aways eliminate pulled or sagging stitches, and are excellent stabilizers to use on knits, dense embroidery designs and open-weave fabrics.

1. After stitching, trim cut-away stabilizer from the edge of the embroidery. It is best to trim after you unhoop the fabric, using a craft scissors to avoid dulling your good fabric shears.

CUT-AWAY STABILIZER

2. Hold the stabilizer as you let the fabric drape underneath to avoid accidentally cutting into the fabric.

3. Trim the stabilizer about ¼" (6mm) from the design.

   • Trimming too closely may cause the design to pucker at the edges.

   • Leaving too much stabilizer will cause an indentation on the right side of the fabric around the design.

Tear-Away Stabilizer

Tear-aways support fabric during embroidery. After stitching is completed, the excess stabilizer is torn away from the design. Tear-aways are great for woven fabrics with body and for use with dense stitching where tearing won't distort the embroidery stitches or the fabric.

1. Place tear-away stabilizer on the wrong side of the fabric.

2. After embroidering, place your thumb on the edge of the embroidery stitches as you tear away the stabilizer.

   • This will alleviate unnecessary and damaging stress on the stitches and the fabric, plus you will get a closer removal of the stabilizer.

3. Remove mutiple layers of stabilizer separately to minimize stress on the stitches.

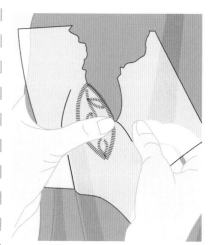

TEAR-AWAY STABILIZER

NOTE *from* NANCY

Another option is to consider choosing a fusible tear-away stabilizer. The fusible application is light and acts as a temporary bond like pinning, and the stabilizer easily tears away.

Wash-Away Stabilizer

Use wash-away stabilizers only on washable fabrics. They are available as a transparent film, a nonwoven fabric-like material or a soluble paper. They may be hooped with the fabric and are easily removed with water.

1 Place a wash-away stabilizer underneath the fabric and/or as a topper stabilizer, which is ideal for napped fabrics and knits.

2 Remove excess stabilizer after embroidery. Tear thin films; otherwise cut away the excess.

3 Use one of these methods for removing the remaining stabilizer:

- Soak heavyweight wash-away stabilizers in water.

- Mist lightweight wash-away stabilizers using a spray bottle.

- Massage adhesive wash-away stabilizers under warm running water.

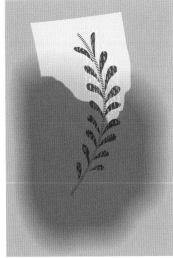

WASH-AWAY STABILIZER

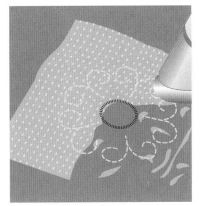

HEAT-AWAY STABILIZER

Heat-Away Stabilizer

Temporary, heat-sensitive stabilizers are there when you need them and then disintegrate with heat from your iron. Use on fabrics that aren't washable (such as velvet, satin and some corduroy), with special techniques like making lace and with delicate fabrics.

1 Place the heat-away stabilizer on the wrong side of fabric.

2 After embroidering, press from the wrong side.

NOTE *from* NANCY

When removing heat-away stabilizer, don't be alarmed when the stabilizer melts. It forms little balls that can be brushed away. Keep a toothbrush dedicated to sewing nearby to easily brush away the residue.

Liquids and Sprays

Most liquids and sprays are used in addition to other stabilizers. They add just a touch more body to the fabric for beautifully stitched embroidery. I like to use Perfect Sew liquid when an area needs to be especially crisp. Regular spray starch is also an option, but I prefer starch alternatives because of their eco-friendly properties.

Starch Alternative

S

Staystitching is a basic technique that has stood the test of time.

Straight stitch on a single layer of fabric ½" (13mm) from the edge when your project calls for ⅝" (16mm) seam allowances to stabilize curves such as necklines, hiplines or waistlines. This stitching is generally recommended following cutting to prevent the area from stretching from overhandling the fabric.

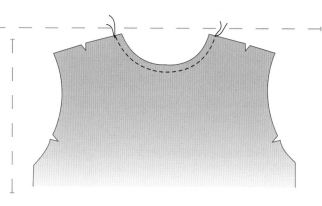

Strata

S

Strata is the term used to describe numerous strips of fabric sewn together along the lengthwise edges. Even though 2"–3" (5cm–8cm) wide strips are commonly stitched together and then subcut into smaller sections, any size strips can create a strata. Regardless of the initial strip size, use the same piecing and pressing technique.

1 Form strip groupings according to the completed block design.

2 Stitch strips into stratas.

- Set the stitch length to 12–15 stitches per inch (per 2.5cm), slightly shorter than normal. Because the strips will be recut, a shorter stitch length makes stitching more secure.

- Join edges with ¼" (6mm) seams, right sides together.

WRONG SIDE

NOTE *from* NANCY

To help stitch accurate ¼" (6mm) seams, I like to use the Little Foot. The right toe of the foot is exactly ¼" (6mm) wide. If I position the right edge of the foot along the cut edges of my strips, I get precise, uniform seams every time.

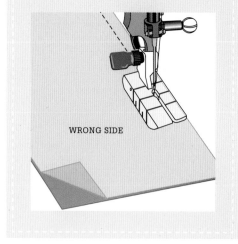

WRONG SIDE

3 Press seams in one direction, generally toward the darker fabric.

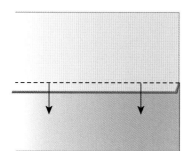

4 Repeat to finish strata.

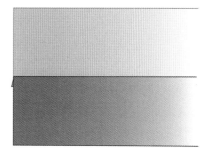

Tension

Balanced stitches are generally easy to achieve if the sewing machine is properly threaded. There may be times that the top thread and bobbin thread are not in sync, causing the seam to pucker or the seam strength to be weak.

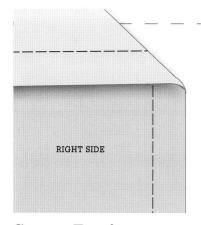

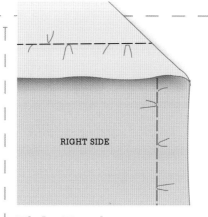

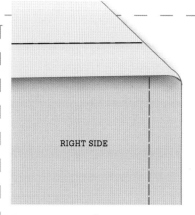

Correct Tension

The stitches look even in length. The bobbin thread color does not appear on the top of the seam, nor does the upper thread color appear on the underside of the seam.

Tight Tension

The fabric puckers and the stitches easily pop when tension is applied to the seam. Slightly loosen the top tension setting and possibly lengthen the stitch.

Loose Tension

The top thread appears on the underside of the seam and the seam is weak. First, check to see if the bobbin thread is properly in the bobbin case and/or guided through the bobbin tension. If the bobbin thread was correctly inserted in the machine, slightly tighten the top tension.

NOTE *from* NANCY

If I'm having difficulty with the stitch tension, my first step is to rethread the machine and check the bobbin case. Nine out of ten times, rethreading solves tension or stitch issues.

T

Choose thread for your project that is the correct weight and a similar fiber content, especially when durability is a consideration. Also consider the design elements of the project, colorations and techniques.

Thread Composition

Thread is made from natural fibers, regenerated fibers or manmade fibers.

- **Natural fibers** include cotton, wool and silk and are produced from plant or animal by-products.

- **Regenerated fibers** such as rayon are derived from plants, but chemicals are used in the process of making the thread.

- **Manmade fibers** are made from minerals or synthetics and include threads such as metallic, polyester and nylon.

Thread is produced in different weights, various size spools and a wide array of colors. The most common weight is 40. The higher the number, the finer the thread. For example, 80 wt. cotton thread is recommended for heirloom sewing, while 12 wt. thread is used for decorative serger stitching. Filaments may be long, short or a combination. Manufacturers choose just the right mixture and amount of fibers to twist together to make thread for various end uses.

A good quality thread sews well—it is durable, abrasion resistant, colorfast and free from knots, slubs and kinks. If possible, it is also guaranteed by the manufacturer.

NOTE *from* NANCY

The most important thing to remember when purchasing thread is to stay away from the bargain bins—buy a good quality thread with no loose fibers. A better sewing experience, a well-running sewing machine and a colorful and durable project will be your rewards.

Topstitching is a stitch sewn on top of the fabric for a decorative appearance on things like pockets, collars and seams. It adds a custom accent and enhances the stability of garment edges.

1 Use double threads in the needle. Place two spools of thread on the top of the machine. Stack them on the spool pin so the threads unwind in opposite directions. This prevents the threads from tangling.

2 Use a topstitch needle. The eye of a topstitch needle is a little larger to accommodate the two threads or a heavier-weight thread.

3 Lengthen the stitch to approximately 8 stitches per inch (per 2.5cm).

NOTE *from* NANCY

If both sides of the fabric will show, also wind two threads simultaneously in the bobbin to create a balanced look.

Underlining

Add an extra layer of support to a lightweight fashion fabric by adding a backing fabric, known as an underlining.

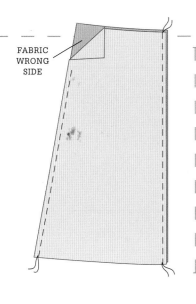

FABRIC WRONG SIDE

1 Cut the underlining the same size as the fashion fabric pattern piece, and machine-baste the underlining to the wrong side of each matching fabric section. Or use a craft glue stick to baste the fabrics together by lightly dabbing along the seam allowance. The glue will dry clear and crisp.

2 Treat the two pieces that have been basted together as one piece of fabric.

NOTE *from* NANCY

An iron-on knit interfacing is a great underlining alternative to use with knit fabrics. Press in position to the wrong side of the fabric to stabilize the knit.

To keep a facing, under collar or under cuff from showing, press and then stitch the seam allowances toward the underside. Understitching prevents the facing from rolling to the right side.

1 Trim and grade the seam allowances.

2 Press the seam flat, then press the facing away from the garment, covering the seam allowance. Press all the seam allowances toward the facing.

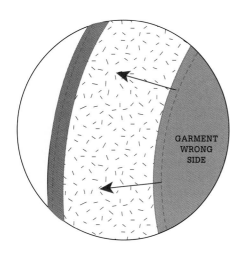

GARMENT
WRONG
SIDE

3 Stitch the seam allowances to the facing, from the right side, with either a straight stitch, zigzag or multi-step zigzag. Stitch on the facing, close to the seamline.

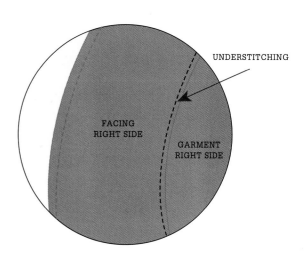

UNDERSTITCHING

FACING
RIGHT SIDE

GARMENT
RIGHT SIDE

NOTE *from* NANCY

Try using a multi-step zigzag for understitching. Instead of just zigzagging back and forth, the machine makes several stitches for each zig and zag. This helps the facing lie smooth. Check your instruction manual to see if your machine can sew this stitch.

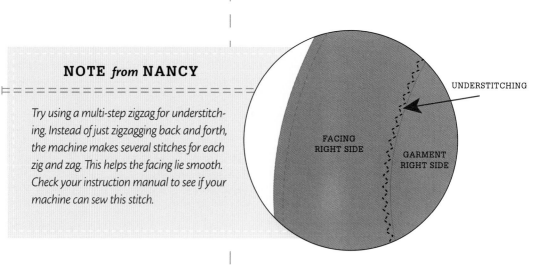

UNDERSTITCHING

FACING
RIGHT SIDE

GARMENT
RIGHT SIDE

Although it's not usually thought of as fabric, vinyl is easy to incorporate into sewing projects. Different types of vinyl include clear, reinforced and traditional. Vinyl is easy to clean—you simply wipe it with a damp cloth. This versatile material doesn't fray, has no grain and is waterproof. It's ideal for crafts, home décor projects and so much more.

Machine Setup

- Use a sharp needle or a topstitch needle, size 90.

- Replace the conventional presser foot with a roller or Teflon foot. This helps feed the fabric smoothly through the machine.

- Adjust stitch length to 3.0mm–3.5mm.

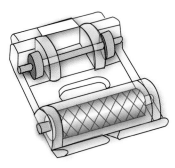

ROLLER FOOT

Sewing Tips

- Stitch with the canvas side (if applicable) under the presser foot.

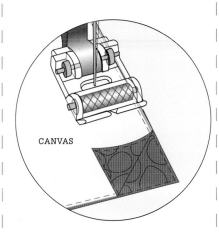

CANVAS

- When topstitching or stitching directly on the vinyl, the fabric may feed unevenly. Place strips of tissue paper on top of and underneath the fabric. Stitch over the tissue paper, then tear away the paper after stitching is completed. The needle will perforate the paper, making it easy to remove.

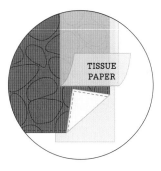

TISSUE PAPER

- Pressing with an iron is not recommended. The heat of the iron could damage the vinyl.

  - Place the vinyl on a flat surface. Finger press or use a Little Wooden Iron to temporarily flatten seams. The seams won't remain open, but this pressing helps shape the seam.

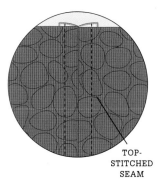

CANVAS   WOODEN IRON

  - Topstitch seam allowances to critical areas such as side seams, stitching down approximately 1"–2" (3cm –5cm) at the top of the seams.

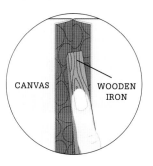

TOP-STITCHED SEAM

A separate waistband on a skirt or pants looks great, but it can add bulk. And who needs more bulk at the waistline? This waistband technique eliminates bulk by removing part of the seam allowance before you cut the band.

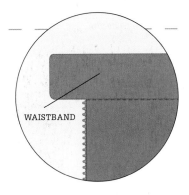

WAISTBAND

1 Insert a zipper in the side or center seam following the pattern instructions or your favorite method. Or, see simple instructions on pages 132–139.

2 Modify and cut out the waistband.

• Fold under ½" (13mm) along the long unnotched edge of the waistband pattern.

Waistband
Cut 1

• Align the folded edge of the waistband pattern along the ravel-free fabric selvage if possible. If you can't place the band on the selvage, finish the edge by zigzagging or serging.

• Cut out the waistband, marking the notches and centers.

3 Interface the waistband.

• Fuse interfacing to the wrong side of the waistband.

• Fold and press the waistband along the foldline with wrong sides together.

4 Stitch the waistband to the garment with right sides together, matching the notches and centers. The waistband will extend beyond the garment on each end.

• Grade the seam allowances, trimming the waistband seam to ¼" (6mm) and the garment seam to ⅜" (10mm).

• To reduce bulk, angle-cut the skirt seam allowances and darts from the stitching line to the cut edge.

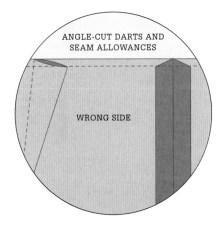

ANGLE-CUT DARTS AND
SEAM ALLOWANCES

WRONG SIDE

• Cut off any excess zipper tape. Securely zigzag over the ends of the zipper tape to reinforce them.

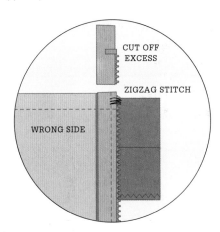

CUT OFF
EXCESS

ZIGZAG STITCH

WRONG SIDE

• Press the seam flat. Then press the waistband up, covering the seam.

5 Fold the waistband along the foldline with right sides together (the lower edges won't meet). The selvage/finished edge extends ⅛" (3mm) below the stitched seamline.

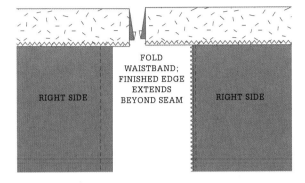

FOLD WAISTBAND; FINISHED EDGE EXTENDS BEYOND SEAM

RIGHT SIDE

RIGHT SIDE

6 Finish the waistband ends.

- Stitch the end seams. On the left end, stitch straight up from the zipper overlap. The right end extends beyond the zipper. Stitch, using a conventional seam allowance.

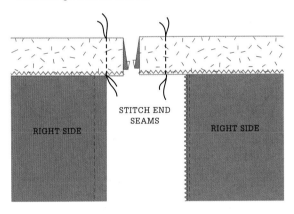

STITCH END SEAMS

RIGHT SIDE

RIGHT SIDE

- Trim and grade the seam allowances. Angle-cut the corners.
- Turn the waistband right-side-out. The selvage/finished edge of the band will extend slightly below the waist seam.

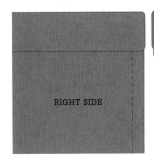

RIGHT SIDE

RIGHT SIDE

7 Turn the waistband right-side-out. Use a tool like a Bamboo Pointer & Creaser to help get sharp corners. Press the band so the foldline is at the top of the band.

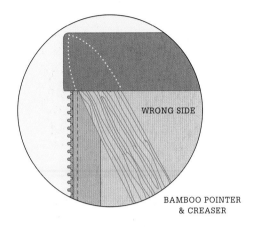

WRONG SIDE

BAMBOO POINTER & CREASER

8 Finish the band.

- Pin the remaining edge of the band over the waist seam. The selvage/finished edge of the band will extend slightly below the waist seam. Pin from the right side of the garment.

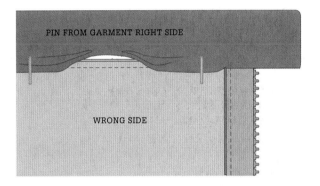

PIN FROM GARMENT RIGHT SIDE

WRONG SIDE

- Stitch in the ditch, stitching from the right side. Straight stitch in the groove (called the ditch) of the seam. The stitching will blend into the seam and will not be noticeable from the right side. On the wrong side, the stitching will catch the remaining waistband edge.

STITCH IN THE DITCH

RIGHT SIDE

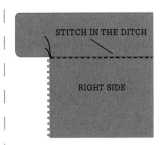

WRONG SIDE

A wrapped corner definitely is a staple in my sewing repertoire. Whenever I stitch a collar, cuff, lapel, pillow or other project with corners where two seams cross, I use this two-step process instead of pivoting at each corner. Try it!

Collars

Although we illustrate a collar, you can use the same process when working with cuffs, lapels and similar edges.

1 Interface the collars. With lightweight fabrics, you may want to interface both the upper and the lower collars. With heavy-weight fabrics, you may prefer to interface only one section. It's your choice.

- Choose a lightweight interfacing. Use the garment pattern to cut the interfacing. It's not necessary to remove interfacing seam allowances if you choose an appropriate weight of interfacing.

- Fuse the interfacing to the wrong side of the fashion fabric following manufacturer's instructions.

WRONG SIDE

2 Meet the under and upper collars, right sides together. Stitch the unnotched edge from end to end.

3 Grade the seam allowances, trimming the under collar to approximately ¼" (6mm) and the upper collar to ⅜" (10mm).

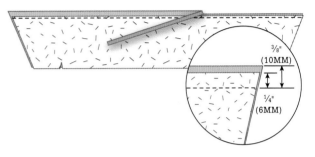

⅜"
(10MM)

¼"
(6MM)

4 Press the seam flat. Then press both seam allowances toward the under collar.

5 Understitch the entire seam with a multi-zigzag, stitching the seam allowance to the under collar.

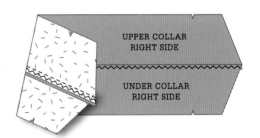

UPPER COLLAR
RIGHT SIDE

UNDER COLLAR
RIGHT SIDE

NOTE *from* NANCY

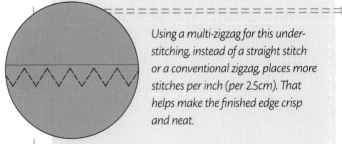

Using a multi-zigzag for this under-stitching, instead of a straight stitch or a conventional zigzag, places more stitches per inch (per 2.5cm). That helps make the finished edge crisp and neat.

6 Fold the collar along the first stitching line, right sides together. Meet the remaining seam edges.

7 Straight stitch from the fold to the neckline edge on each end of the collar.

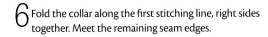

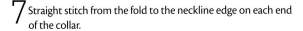

8 Grade the seam allowances. Angle-cut the corners.

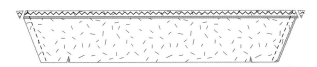

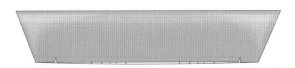

9 Press the collar and turn it right-side-out. Use a Bamboo Pointer & Creaser or awl to help get uniform accurate points.

Intersecting Seams

Use the same wrapped-corner technique to get sharp, crisp edges on other seams that intersect, such as cuffs and pillows, instead of pivoting.

1 Pin fabrics, right sides together. Stitch one seam, sewing from edge to edge.

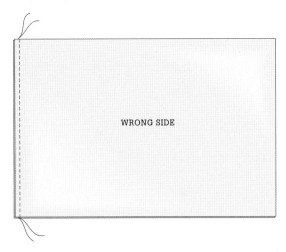

WRONG SIDE

2 Press along the stitching line, folding the seam toward the interior of the project.

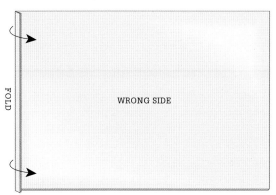

FOLD

WRONG SIDE

3 Stitch the adjacent seams, sewing from the fold to the fabric edge.

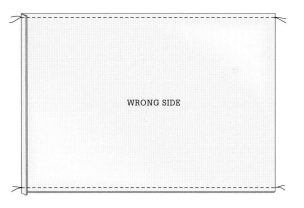

WRONG SIDE

4 Turn the project right-side-out.

Y

What's old often becomes new again. That's certainly the case with fabric yo-yos. During the 1930s and 1940s, sewers and quilters cut scraps of fabric into circles, gathered them into yo-yo-like puffs and sewed them together into coverlets.

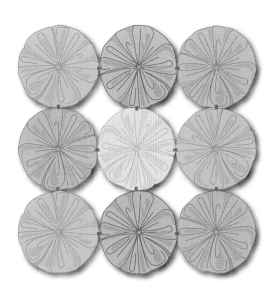

Traditional Yo-Yos

In the past, women traced canning jar lids or other circular objects onto fabric, cut them out and carried them with them wherever they went so they could stitch during free moments. Here's the technique they used to make their yo-yos.

1 Cut out a fabric circle. The finished yo-yo will be approximately one-third to one-half the size of the cut-out circle, so adjust the circle size accordingly.

2 Fold under ¼" (6mm) along the edges of the circle and hand-stitch around the circle.

- Thread a hand sewing needle with a doubled length of thread. Knot the thread, leaving a ½"–1" (13mm–25mm) thread tail beyond the knot. This makes it easier to see the starting point when you're completing the yo-yo.

- Sew a gathering stitch around the outer edges of the circle.

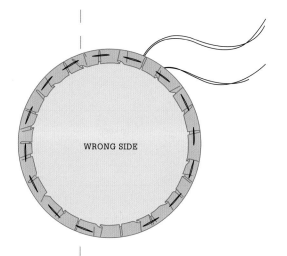

WRONG SIDE

3 Pull the threads and gather the circle into a little puff, with the outer edges gathered together in the center.

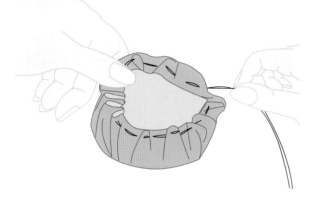

4 Adjust the gathering until the yo-yo has the shape you want. A small hole forms in the middle.

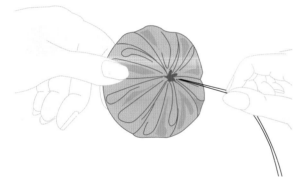

5 Flatten the yo-yo and center the hole. Tie the threads to keep the gathers in place; trim the excess thread.

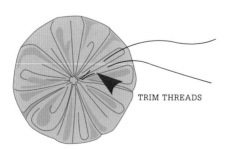

TRIM THREADS

6 Place the yo-yos edge to edge and whip stitch them together.

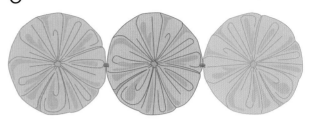

NOTE *from* NANCY

It's easier to shape the yo-yo and knot the thread if you place it on a padded board.

NOTE *from* NANCY

There's an even easier way to make yo-yos. Use Clover's Yo-Yo Maker, a two-part product consisting of a plate and disk. The fabric fits between the two parts. You'll find openings for the hand stitching, taking all the guesswork out of the process. (The packaging provides full instructions.) If you're making a large quantity of yo-yos, this might be a smart investment.

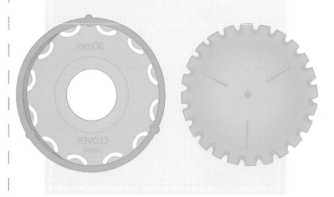

Z

Second only to a straight stitch, the zigzag stitch is a sewing mainstay.

The zigzag stitch is a common stitch used to finish seam edges and apply appliqués.

The multi-zigzag is a variation of the zigzag stitch formed by three stitches in each direction. It is often used when a stretch stitch or understitching is recommended.

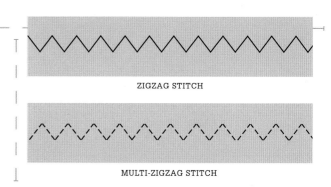

ZIGZAG STITCH

MULTI-ZIGZAG STITCH

Zippers

Z

Zippers may seem intimidating, but don't avoid projects that feature them. Use one of my favorite techniques for a centered, lapped, invisible or exposed zipper. These easy-to-sew methods make sewing zippers fun and fast.

Getting Ready

1 Purchase a zipper about 2" (5cm) longer than the pattern recommends.

- With the longer length, you won't have trouble stitching around the bulky zipper pull.

2 Decide whether you will use a centered zipper or a lapped zipper. Follow the directions for the one you choose.

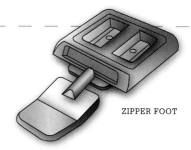

ZIPPER FOOT

3 Attach a zipper foot.

- Your zipper foot may not look exactly like the one pictured. Check your machine's instruction manual if you need help identifying the foot.

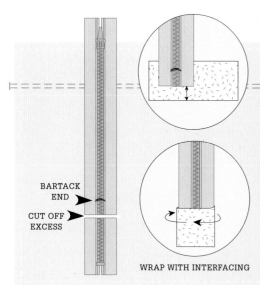

BARTACK END

CUT OFF EXCESS

WRAP WITH INTERFACING

NOTE *from* NANCY

I like to have zippers on hand, so generally I buy a variety of colors whenever I see them on sale. My rule of thumb is to purchase the longest size available—it's extremely easy to shorten them.

Shortening a Zipper

- Set the machine to a medium-width zigzag and 0 stitch length.
- Bartack a new zipper stop; cut off the excess tape.
- Soften the cut end of the zipper by wrapping it with fusible interfacing. Press into position.

Centered Zipper

A centered zipper is easy to insert. Two lines of straight stitching show on the right side of the fabric. A centered zipper is preferred at center front openings and is sometimes used at back openings.

1 Baste the zipper opening with right sides together. Permanently stitch the rest of the seam, and press the seam open.

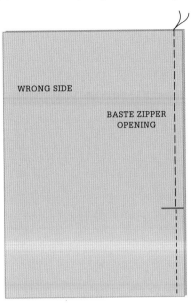

2 Center the zipper over the pressed seam allowance.

- Put the right side of the zipper next to the seam allowance. The lower edge of the zipper teeth should be at the end of the zipper opening. The pull tab will extend past the top of the fabric.

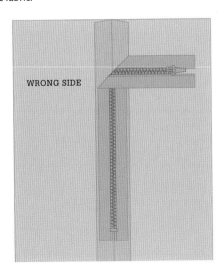

3 Use strips of ½" (13mm) wide tape, such as Sewer's Fix-It Tape, to hold the zipper to the seam allowance.

- Tape the top and bottom of the zipper. Add one or two more tape strips in the middle of the zipper, depending on the zipper's length.

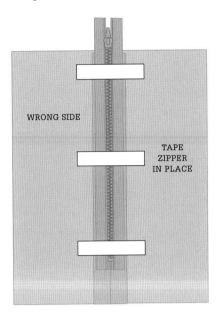

4 Turn the project right-side-out. Center another piece of ½" (13mm) tape over the zipper seamline. The same amount of tape should extend on each side of the seam.

5 Stitch across the bottom and up one side of the zipper, following the edge of the tape as a guide.

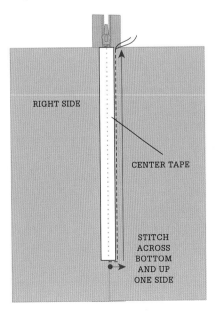

continued on next page >

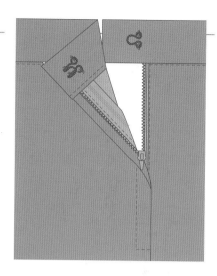

6
Repeat, stitching across the bottom and up the other side of the zipper.

- You may have to reposition the zipper foot or adjust the needle position.

- Check your machine's instruction manual if you need help.

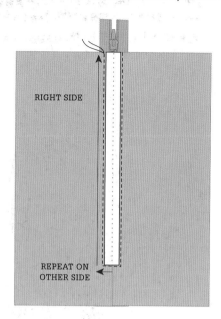

RIGHT SIDE

REPEAT ON OTHER SIDE

7
Remove the tape on the outside and inside of the project. Remove the basting stitches.

8
Pull the zipper tab down within the zipper opening. Set the stitch length to 0. Zigzag several times (bartack) across the upper ends of the zipper teeth so the pull won't come off. The extra zipper tape can be cut off after the top of the opening is finished with a facing or waistband.

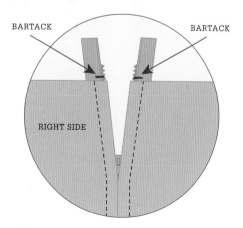

BARTACK   BARTACK

RIGHT SIDE

Lapped Zipper

A lapped zipper gives a tailored look. Only one line of stitching shows on the right side of the fabric. It's easier to keep the stitching straight and to make sure the zipper teeth are completely covered. I prefer the lapped zipper for side openings and sometimes back openings.

1
Before cutting out your garment, increase the zipper seam allowance to 1" (25mm).

- For example, if the pattern allows a ⅝" (16mm) seam allowance, add ⅜" (10mm) to the seam in the zipper area.

2
Mark the 1" (25mm) seamline at the top of the zipper opening on both the left and right seam allowances. These markings are very important.

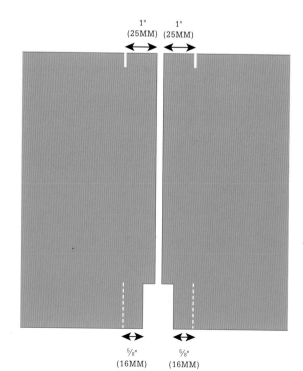

1" (25MM)   1" (25MM)

⅝" (16MM)   ⅝" (16MM)

3 Stitch the seam below the zipper opening, stopping at the dot that marks the zipper opening and its wider seam allowance. Lock your stitches at the dot by sewing in place several times with the machine's stitch length set at 0.

4 Press the seam.

- Press the seam open below the zipper opening.

- On the garment's left side, fold and press under the entire 1" (25mm) seam allowance in the zipper area. Use the marking and the lower end of the zipper opening to position the foldline.

- On the garment's right side, press under ⅞" (22mm) of the 1" (25mm) seam allowance to create the zipper underlay. The finished zipper will lap left over right.

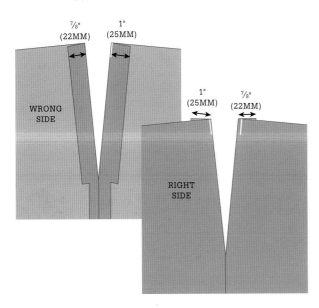

5 Insert the zipper.

- With right-sides-up, position the closed zipper under the zipper underlay with the bottom of the zipper at the base of the zipper opening. Place the underlay fold next to the right side of the zipper teeth. Make certain the zipper tab extends above the top of the garment. With short zippers, you shouldn't have to pin the zipper—you can merely finger pin and stitch.

- Position the machine's zipper foot to the left of the needle. Stitch next to the fold, from the bottom to the top.

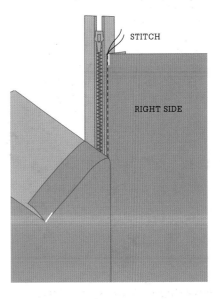

- Lap the left side of the garment over its right side, matching the markings. Tape the overlap in place.

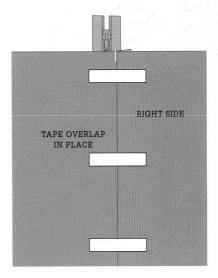

NOTE *from* NANCY

Pins sometimes create dimples in the fabric, causing uneven stitching. Instead of pins, use strips of Sewer's Fix-It Tape about 4" (10cm) apart to position the lap. This ½" (13mm) wide tape keeps the edge perfectly flat and results in more even topstitching. When you're finished, you can easily remove the tape, leaving no sticky residue.

continued on next page >

6 Topstitch the overlap.

- Align a strip of ½" (13mm) wide Sewer's Fix-It Tape or transparent tape along the folded edge of the lapped seam allowance. This provides an accurate stitching guide.

- Slide the zipper foot to the right of the needle.

- Beginning at the base of the zipper, topstitch along the bottom edge of the tape and up the side.

- Remove the tape.

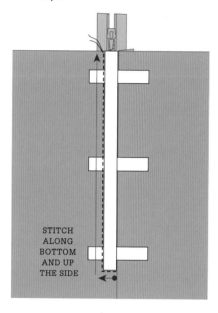

STITCH
ALONG
BOTTOM
AND UP
THE SIDE

7 Complete the zipper insertion.

- Move the zipper pull down into the completed zipper placket. Satin stitch or bartack over the ends of the zipper tape at the top of the zipper reinforcement.

- Cut off the excess zipper tape.

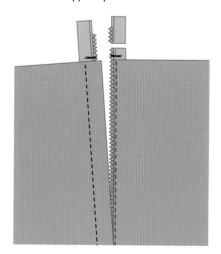

Invisible Zipper

An invisible zipper is a special type of zipper designed to look like a seam when closed. You can insert an invisible zipper in side seams, center back seams or center front seams, or you can use an invisible zipper when creating home decor items.

Note: The following instructions are for a center back opening. They can easily be adapted for other openings.

1 Prepare the zipper opening and the facing.

- Do not stitch the seam closed. The entire seam remains open during the zipper insertion.

- Mark the ⅝" (16mm) seam allowances for the zipper opening on the right side of both garment sections. This identifies where to position the zipper teeth during zipper application.

⅝" (16MM)

NOTE *from* NANCY

Most tape measures are ⅝" (16mm) wide, so you can easily transfer that marking by simply placing the edge of a tape measure along the fabric's cut edge. Then mark along the opposite edge of the tape measure using a water-soluble pen or chalk.

- Trim ⅝" (16mm) from the center back of both facings. A smaller facing later causes the garment seam allowance to wrap around the zipper.

⅝" (16MM)

2 Insert the invisible zipper.

- Press the zipper to flatten the zipper coils—the most important step! Doing so makes insertion easier. One word of caution: Use a cool temperature setting. Since the coils are usually made of nylon or polyester, too much heat can damage them.

- Attach an invisible zipper foot. This special foot glides over the fabric and the zipper.

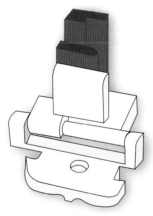

INVISIBLE ZIPPER FOOT

- Open the zipper. With right sides together, place the zipper so one taped edge is even with the edge of one back seam allowance and the zipper teeth are at the marked seamline.

MARKED SEAMLINE

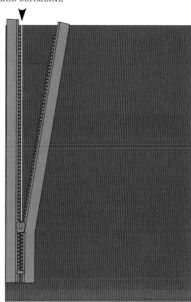

- Stitch next to the zipper teeth from top to bottom. You will not be able to stitch completely to the bottom of the zipper; a short section remains unstitched.

- Close the zipper. Pin the unstitched side of the zipper to the remaining back seam allowance with right sides together. This ensures that the two sides of the garment will meet on the finished application. Open the zipper and stitch the second side of the zipper.

WRONG SIDE

continued on next page >

3 Close the seam at the bottom of the zipper.

- Replace the invisible zipper foot with a conventional zipper foot.

- Reposition the zipper foot to the left of the needle.

- Meet the garment seam edges below the zipper with right sides together. Stitch the seam, overlapping a few stitches at the bottom of the zipper.

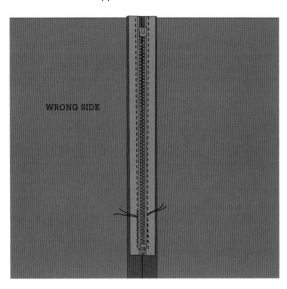

WRONG SIDE

4 Attach the facing.

- Stitch the front facing to the back facing at the shoulder seams with right sides together.

- Pin the facing to the garment at the center back with right sides together. Stitch a ¼" (6mm) seam at each center back edge.

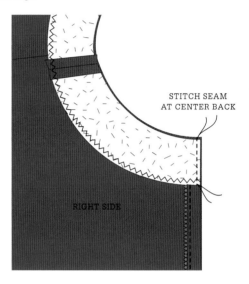

STITCH SEAM
AT CENTER BACK

RIGHT SIDE

- Meet the facing to the neckline with right sides together, matching the shoulder seams. Pin. Since the facing is smaller than the garment, the garment wraps around the zipper with the zipper teeth at the fold.

- Stitch the neckline seam.

- Grade and trim the seam. Understitch the seam allowances.

- Turn the facing to the wrong side.

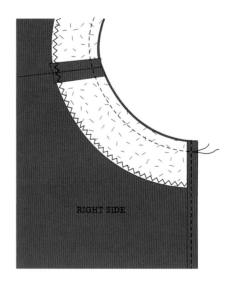

RIGHT SIDE

Exposed Zipper

This is an extremely easy method for inserting a zipper. It's especially useful for making bags. If you're using fabrics that don't ravel, such as oilcloth, you don't even need to finish the edges. How's that for easy?

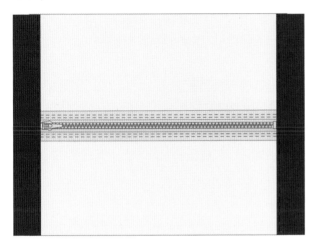

1 If necessary, finish the seam edges by serging or zigzagging to prevent raveling.

2 Position the zipper along one finished edge, meeting the wrong side of the zipper to the right side of the fabric. Make sure that the fabric is a scant ¼" (6mm) away from the zipper teeth to allow room for opening and closing the zipper. Stitch.

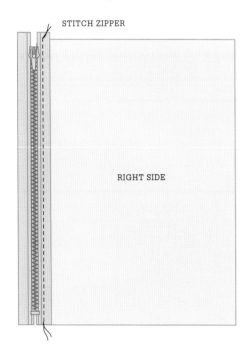

STITCH ZIPPER

RIGHT SIDE

3 Add a second line of stitching close to the first stitching to reinforce the zipper.

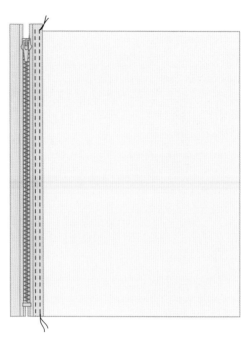

4 Repeat, stitching the zipper to the opposite edge of the fabric.

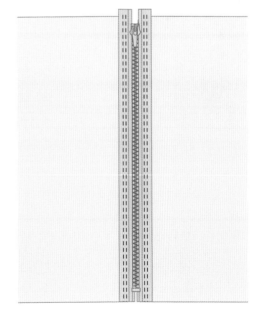

Visit these manufacturers' websites for more information on the tools and supplies mentioned in the book, as well as many other great notions that will help you on your sewing and quilting journey!

Clover Needlecraft, Inc.
www.clover-usa.com

EZ Quilting by Wrights
www.ezquilt.com

Fasturn, LLC
www.fasturn.net

OLFA
www.olfa.com

Oliso Irons
www.oliso.com

Pellon Consumer Products
www.pellonideas.com

Prym Consumer USA, Inc.
www.dritz.com

Rowenta Irons
www.rowenta.com

The Sewing Revolution
www.thesewingrevolution.com.au

Wrights
www.wrights.com

Keep Sewing with Nancy!

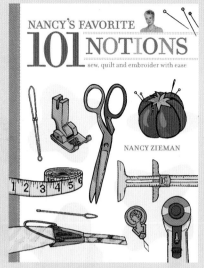

Stash with Splash Quilts

Cindy Casciato and Nancy Zieman

All quilters have a fabric stash that they don't know how to use. Author Cindy Casciato gives you inspiring quilt patterns to showcase your stash fabrics with a zinger fabric thrown in for splash. Learn time-saving techniques and receive tips from quilting expert Nancy Zieman. An included DVD steps you through a variety of techniques and projects. You'll love combining stash with splash to make these gorgeous quilts!

PAPERBACK / 128 PAGES + DVD

Nancy's Favorite 101 Notions

Nancy Zieman

For the past 25 years, Nancy Zieman has offered innovative ideas, inspiration and information designed to make sewing, serging, quilting and embroidering more efficient—and more enjoyable. Now she offers a guidebook to every tool you'll ever need! Nancy describes the features of each tool—so you can find a tool that works, regardless of brand—and details the various uses. With *Nancy's Favorite 101 Notions*, you can find the tools that will make sewing easier, faster, more creative and more fun!

PAPERBACK / 128 PAGES

Piece in the Hoop

Larisa Bland and Nancy Zieman

Turn your embroidery machine into a block-piecing machine! With Larisa's designs, you can piece in the hoop™! All you have to do is add fabric and flip—the embroidery machine does all the sewing for you—resulting in fast, precise blocks every time. An included DVD and advice from Nancy Zieman make this method even easier and more fun!

PAPERBACK / 128 PAGES + DVD

These and other fine Krause Publications titles are available at your local craft retailer, bookstore or online supplier, or visit our website at
www.mycraftivitystore.com.